Angie's Story

as told to Barbara G. Appelbaum
and Peter Marchant

Center for Holocaust Awareness and Information (CHAI)
Jewish Community Federation of Greater Rochester, New York

ISBN
0-9710686-4-X (Cloth)
0-9710686-5-8 (Paper)

First U.S. Edition

Published in the United States of America
2003 by the Jewish Community Federation
of Greater Rochester, New York
441 East Avenue, Rochester, NY 14607

(585) 461-0490
www.jewishrochester.org

*I dedicate this book to
the memory of my parents, David and Lea Szpilman,
my brother, Motus, and my thirty-six aunts, uncles and cousins
who were murdered during the Holocaust.*

*To my dear husband Jacob Suss,
who also survived, but died in the prime of his life.*

*With love to my sons, David and Ted,
and their families, whom I hope will
remember and continue to tell my story,
and to my sister Barbara who survived with me.*

*In memory of my dear friend Henry Shweid,
who always wanted to hear my story.*

Table of Contents

Acknowledgments

This book could not have become a reality without the inspiration, active participation and contributions of many people. We would like to thank all the teachers and their students who encouraged Angie to speak and share her story. They touched her heart as she touched theirs. We are particularly indebted to the students and faculty at Gates Chili Middle School who first gave voice to the idea of this book. Thanks also to David, Ted and Jake Suss for their essays and to Barbara Mand, Angie's sister, and the entire Suss family. We also wish to thank Ted for his assistance with the photographs and the cover design. We appreciate Martin Rumscheidt's sharing his reflections with us.

We are most grateful to the Foundation for the Jewish Community for its support and to The Jewish Community Federation of Greater Rochester and the Center for Holocaust Awareness and Information (CHAI) for guidance in creating this resource.

We are indebted to the Jewish Heritage Project and Alan Adelson for his advice and for permission to draw freely from his book *Lodz Ghetto: Inside a Community Under Siege.* Thanks to the staff at the United States Holocaust Memorial Museum for their assistance, with special thanks to Leslie Swift and Judy Cohen at the Photo Archives and Martin Goldman, Director of Survivor Affairs.

Many people at SUNY Brockport made important contributions. We are indebted to Kim Scott for her beautiful graphic design and her patience through endless revisions. Thanks also to William Heyen for his support and permission to use his poems, "Fugue for Angie" and "Angel" in this book. Judith Kitchen's editorial suggestions were invaluable. We thank her for the confidence she showed in the book.

Thanks to Nazareth professor, Dr. Susan Nowak and her students in the *Auschwitz and After* class. In particular we want to recognize: Deborah DiFilippo for allowing us to use her inspiring collage *Angie's Story* on the book's cover and her reflection; to Kelly Ceckowski for her photograph of the memorial candle she lit at Auschwitz; and to Sarah Cudzilo for her research and notes.

We appreciate the editorial assistance provided by Brian Moore, Barbara Lovenheim and Dana Logsdon. Dana, Peter's former student and now colleague at Brockport, provided invaluable help in bringing this book to its conclusion. In addition to writing the photo credits, she spent many hours assisting with the final revisions.

Thanks to Anthony Giardina who devoted himself to creating a CD-ROM for students to use with the book and to RIT Professors Nancy Doubleday and Stephen Jacobs.

We would like to thank our spouses, Mary Elsie Robertson and E. David Appelbaum, and our families for their encouragement. Above all, we thank Angie for her confidence and patience as we subjected her to hundreds of hours of interviews spanning many years. We hope this book does justice to her story.

Preface

For the past sixteen years Angie Suss Paull has been my frequent companion as we have traveled thousands of miles speaking to students in their classrooms. She is one of a dozen Holocaust survivors in the greater Rochester, New York, area who share their personal stories with students. As Director of the Center for Holocaust Awareness and Information, I have the privilege of experiencing first-hand the powerful impact Angie's testimonies make on student audiences. She can, for example, hold an assembly of 300 eighth graders spellbound for over an hour while she recounts how she saved her sister's life during a selection at Auschwitz, how she sabotaged bullets when forced to work in a German ammunition factory, and how, after liberation, she had to sneak across borders to return to Poland searching for surviving family members.

This stylishly dressed woman, with short gray hair, always perfectly groomed, could be their grandmother. She has a wonderful way of connecting with students and letting them know that she was an ordinary teenager, just like them, leading an ordinary life in a close loving family. Suddenly, she had to find a way of coping with ghettos and concentration camps under unimaginable circumstances. She urges students not to tell racist jokes nor to make fun of those who are different, but to value every human being; she is living proof of where prejudice can lead. Angie also warns people of the danger of being consumed with bitterness. Hate is a waste of time.

The thousands of letters she receives attest to the effectiveness of Angie's words. After hearing her story, many realize they must not take their own families or comfortable lives for granted. She gives students courage to face their own problems. If she could survive four years of starvation and grueling labor in the Lodz Ghetto, if she could face Auschwitz and Bergen-Belsen, perhaps they can overcome their challenges.

For decades people avoided hearing the eyewitness testimony of Holocaust survivors as the Holocaust was relegated to no more than a paragraph in history textbooks. Those who had seen the photos and newsreels of recently liberated concentration camps with the emaciated bodies of survivors, barely alive, were traumatized. Even today they cannot deal with the subject. This lack of interest in her suffering proved very painful to Angie as she relates in her Prologue.

What a contrast today as teachers, recognizing how much students can learn from these important witnesses, eagerly invite survivors into their classrooms. And Angie, and those like her, can memorialize their families as they educate and warn people that this should never happen again, thereby finding meaning and purpose in their lives.

It is our hope that this book will preserve Angie's story and portray this unique period in history when survivors have became powerful educators. To that end Professor Peter Marchant began recording Angie's experiences in depth. Although many others had taken her oral history, something magical happened under Peter's prodding and detailed questioning, his empathy and sense of narrative. Angie began to remember more and more details, even the dress that she and her sister wore to their brother's Bar Mitzvah. Story followed story in endless succession.

Such detailed retelling of her story took its toll on Angie. Speaking to students for forty-five minutes to an hour, she could paint her story with broad brush stokes, giving an overview of her experiences. At some presentations there were tears, and sometimes, when she was feeling especially vulnerable, she would break down, especially when she related how her mother was shipped away from the family in the Lodz Ghetto, or how her father and brother were killed shortly after their arrival in Auschwitz. But for the most part Angie was able to maintain some distance from the history she shared.

Now, with Peter's endless questions, the memories came flooding back and with them a heightened sense of loss. Tears were shed more frequently, and at times it was very painful. Thankfully she persevered.

After Peter sketched out the narrative as far as he could go, I sat down with Angie and she told her story again, filling in more and more details as we amplified, corrected and refined what Peter had done. Old stories expanded and new ones were shared. A whole world opened up to me.

From time to time Angie checked with her sister Barbara, who filled in some important details, especially how they commemorated Yom Kippur at Bergen-Belsen. It took us an entire summer to complete the process. Then I proceeded to blend my narrative with Peter's and, following the advice of Bill Heyen, tried to preserve as much of Angie's voice as possible.

We hope what has emerged is true to Angie's memories and her voice. We are grateful to her for her endless patience as we struggled to understand events that even those who experienced them have difficulty understanding.

We trust that this twice-told story reflects Angie, her courage, her resilience, her uncanny ability to adapt to events as they unfolded. We hope to show how her youth, her optimism, her refusal to give up all worked in her favor. Her strong and loving family life prior to the Holocaust gave her a solid grounding. Luck certainly came into play – as did many miracles.

We were amazed at the picture of Angie that emerged - always struggling to maintain a measure of civilization in the midst of the most appalling conditions. To relieve the boredom and monotony of long evenings in the ghetto, she used her knitting skills to make herself an outfit from a worn-out pair of her father's long underwear. When she was about to leave Bergen-Belsen for Salzwedel to work in the ammunition factory, she made another outfit from the second-hand clothes they issued her. Once in Salzwedel, she used the needle she was given and, taking thread from her blanket, cut down her long blue-striped prisoner coat to create a hat that would keep her warm. Her practical wisdom guided her; her sister's presence and companionship sustained her.

In detailing the many stories of Angie and her husband Jacob in the United States, we tried to follow the advice of Martin Goldman, Director of Survivor Affairs, at the United States Holocaust Memorial Museum. He stressed the importance of conveying survivors' experiences post Holocaust, of relating how they built new lives for themselves, marrying, trying to raise children who would not be scarred by their parents' experiences.

There is so much beauty in the relationship of Angie and Jake, their meeting, their marriage, and the details of their wedding. Once in the United States, Jake, who had every reason to accept the assistance of others, remained fiercely independent, wanting to make it in America with his own hard work. Later on, Jake left a thriving business in Manhattan to move to Rochester and begin anew so that Angie could live close to her sister.

Angie was determined that her children lead a normal life. Above all, she did not want them to hate, even those who had made her family suffer. When her younger son Ted chose to study German as his foreign language in public school, she knew she had succeeded.

We hope this book will give the reader a sense of the tremendous impact Angie has made on others. The Epilogue tells the story of Angie's friendship with Kelly Ceckowski, a former Nazareth College student. Kelly went to Eastern Europe when Angie could not and lit a candle in Auschwitz to help Angie mourn the loss of her family. Kelly was engaging in *tikkun olam*, an attempt to heal the world.

Another former Nazareth College student, Deborah DiFilippo, created the artwork that graces the book's cover. We include her moving reflections. The Afterword tells how Angie's testimony affected Martin Rumscheidt who, like William Heyen, has struggled with his German heritage and the active participation of some family members in what happened during the Holocaust.

We conclude with some personal comments from those closest to Angie – her sons and grandson – and Peter's response.

As this book was going to press, Angie celebrated another milestone, the birth of her first great grandchild. Mackenzie Abigail was born to David's daughter Julie on August 28, 2003. Angie knit Mackenzie a layette and sent her a heart-shaped gold ring. And so a fourth generation begins. Like her mother and Angie's two other granddaughters, she will continue a tradition that began in the Lodz Ghetto when Angie's father David exchanged his meager food rations for scraps of gold so he could have a heart-shaped ring fabricated to give her on her 21st birthday.

Barbara G. Appelbaum

Prologue

When Jake and I came to America in December 1947, our baby David was six months old. No one wanted to hear stories about the Holocaust. When people asked me, "How are you?" I didn't know that in the United States you are supposed to answer, "Fine, thank you." Instead I would begin to cry.

Then people would say, "Forget about it. You're in a new country. You have a husband and a baby. Forget about the past. What was, was. Learn the language and go on with your life."

I didn't answer them, but thought, "You are either stupid, dumb or ignorant. If you had lost your parents and relatives, would you say forget about it?" There isn't a day that goes by that I don't think about my past, my loved ones who were killed. I try to lead a normal life, but in my heart, I always feel the pain. Only other survivors can understand what we went through. So, for forty years I said nothing.

Then in 1987 there was an exhibit of Auschwitz posters organized by the Jewish Community Federation at Monroe Community College in Rochester. Professor David Day, an anthropologist, was in charge. He invited all the survivors to come to the exhibit to help talk about the posters. We were all reluctant to go, because we still believed that people would not want to listen. We went for another reason, to examine the posters. Maybe we would find some relatives in those photographs.

One day while I stood looking at a poster of the barracks at Auschwitz and the three-tiered bunk beds where we slept five to a bed, I overheard some visitors talking behind me.

"It must have been terrible to sleep under those conditions," one woman remarked to her friend.

"Yes, it was terrible," I turned around and said. "I was there."

Their eyes opened wide. "Please, tell us about it," they urged.

I started to speak and from that day on I have never stopped telling my story. I have been speaking for the past 16 years and will continue until I can't go on anymore. Even when vacationing winters in Palm Springs, California, I continue to speak to students in schools there. In

Rochester I speak to over 3,000 students a year, in many different schools.

I feel God spared me for a reason – to share the many miracles that happened to me and to remember my loved ones.

In 1995, after I had shared my story with a 6th grade class at Gates Chili Middle School, a boy asked me, "Why don't you write a book? You speak in such great detail that I feel I am right there with you."

I had never thought about it. But then I said to myself, "That kid is right. I should write a book."

A year later I started taping my story with Professor Peter Marchant and his daughter Jenny. That was seven years ago. Now I am pleased that students will be able to read my story. I hope that they will learn what really happened to me during the Holocaust and apply its lessons to their own lives – to be good, to help each other, not to make fun of others who are different. They should not just stand by, but stand up for other human beings. Whatever happens to them, they should know that life goes on and they should look forward to a brighter future.

I do not have hate in my heart for anyone; I saw what it does to people. Hate is a waste of time. When you hate someone else, you really hate yourself. Even if we live to be a 120, it is still a short time. So we must respect each other's religion, color or creed. We are all God's children. Why not live in peace?

Angie Suss Paull

Angie with sixth graders from Gates Chili Middle School. Behind her is the memorial wall that students had created for her.
Rochester, NY   June 2000

Angie's Story

*The burning of the Reform Temple on Kosciuszko
Boulevard, on the night of November 14, 1939.*

Fugue for Angie

Around the corner where I lived a beautiful synagogue was burning.
Around the corner where I lived. Around the corner.
A beautiful synagogue. Was burning. Where I lived.
Around the corner where I lived a beautiful synagogue was burning....

My father came home in the evening I didn't recognize him.
He didn't want to talk and didn't talk what happened to him.
Was burning. He didn't want to talk and didn't talk.
What happened to him. A beautiful synagogue where I lived.
He didn't want to talk and didn't talk what happened to him....

Will they kill me is not so easy to forget either.
I didn't recognize him. Came home in the evening.
Around the corner where I live will they kill me. Was burning.
He didn't want to talk. What happened to him.
Will they kill me is not so easy to forget either.
A beautiful synagogue was burning. What happened to him...

We packed the little things what we could carry.
My father said we didn't know where we are going who
will live will die. He didn't want to talk.
My father came home in the evening I didn't recognize him.
Will they kill me. Around the corner where I lived.
What we could carry. We packed. Who will live who
will die. Around the corner a beautiful synagogue....

I didn't recognize him. My father. What happened to him.
Was burning. Will they kill me is not so easy.
The little things what we could carry. Was burning.
Around the corner where I lived a beautiful synagogue was burning.

William Heyen

Klezmer Musicians
So many family members played musical instruments that they formed their own band.

Life before the war

I was born Andzia Szpilman on September 8, 1922, in Lodz, Poland, the second oldest of three children. My sister Bronya was two years older and my brother Motus was two years younger.

I come from a family of klezmer musicians, who played Jewish folk-tunes, primarily at weddings and special festivities. That is how my father's family got its name. "Szpilman" in German means player, performer, or minstrel. So many family members played musical instruments that they formed their own band. I have a photograph from the 1800's that appeared in *The Pictorial History of the Jewish People*. It shows my great grandfather, great uncle, and cousins seated with their musical instruments.

I never met any of these relatives, but my father told me that as a little boy, he loved music so much he would beg my grandfather to let him attend rehearsals. Grandfather would sneak him into the theatre where he would sit for hours on the floor, hidden between rows of chairs, listening to the family rehearse. When he grew up, Father played the drums in a band. He gave up his musical career after he married my mother. She was religious and he no longer wanted to travel with the band or perform on the Sabbath. He looked for a career that would give him more time to spend with the family.

Father had three brothers and two sisters. All but his older sister came to the United States before the First World War. My Uncle Sam was the last to arrive. In 1937 he had a two-month contract to play piano and accordion in Harbin, Uruguay. The audience liked him so much they extended his contract for another two years. By then it was the spring of 1939. He wanted to bring his family back to Poland, but when he wrote to tell my father that he was returning, Father wrote back immediately. "The weather's getting very hot. Join your brothers Max and Izzy and Norma." Father didn't want to mention the United States or Poland in case the mail was censored. He just gave the names of his brothers and sister living in the US. Soon after, Sam was able to enter the United States. Father's letter saved his life.

You may wonder why Father chose to remain in Poland. When he was 17, he had actually received papers to immigrate to the United States and join the family there. Not wanting to leave his mother alone in Lodz, however, he gave the papers to his younger brother Izzy who was 14. Since at that time a photograph wasn't required, Father dressed Izzy in clothes that made him look older, more like a 17 year old. In the United States Izzy eventually became a successful businessman.

Many of my Szpilman cousins were talented in music, but the most famous of them all was Wladyslaw Szpilman. He lived in Warsaw until his death in July 2000. A concert pianist and composer before the war, he played on the Polish radio and in the movies. Then from 1945 to 1963 he was Director of Music at Polish Radio. Wladyslaw survived the war by hiding both within and outside the Warsaw Ghetto. After the ghetto was liquidated, an officer in the German Wehrmacht came upon him playing Chopin on an old piano in the abandoned ghetto and helped him survive. I discovered him in August 1999 when his 1946 memoir was finally published in the United States as *The Pianist.* My son David contacted Wladyslaw and on December 5, 1999, his birthday, I called him and sang him the traditional song.

"You still remember Polish," he said.

Wladyslaw invited me to visit him in Warsaw, but he died before I was able to go.

**Polish Army Band
taken around 1919-1920 after World War I.**

Angie's Uncle Sam Szpilman is in the second row from the back, fourth from the left. At her father's urging Sam did not return to Poland after he had an engagement playing in Uruguay but instead immigrated to the United States in 1939. In 1947 it was Uncle Sam who met Angie, her husband and son at the New York pier when they came to the United States.

Mother and Father's engagement portrait
David Szpilman and Lea Miller, Lodz, 1919

Mother was an orphan. After her parents died, mother, her three brothers and sister went to live with their aunt and uncle. Mother did everything in the house: cleaning, washing, and cooking. She also went into her uncle's retail clothing shop to serve customers. She was so good at selling they kept her there. That's how she learned to be a businesswoman.

Father was in shoe manufacturing. He brought home leather from the factory to make shoe uppers. He cut them and returned them to the factory to be attached to soles.

In this photo mother and father are both 19. When I was 19 I looked like her – not now, of course: I've outlived her by almost 40 years. She was only 44 when she was killed.

I think I take after her in temperament—quick, nervous and expressive. Barbara takes after Father, who was quiet, inclined to keep his worries to himself.

Where and how we lived

Before the war we lived on the second floor of a big apartment building on Nowomiejska 6 Street. With two entrances, one for my parents' business and the other private for our living quarters, the apartment seemed big to us, but by American standards it was small. My brother Motus had his own small room; Barbara and I shared another. The biggest room was my parents' bedroom. I loved that room. I can still see how beautiful it was with its red floor polished so highly that my mother could see her reflection in it. Decorating the walls was a hand-painted garden scene with wild flowers and a pond in the middle. The ceiling was painted blue with stars as if it were dusk.

At the other end of their room stood a big dining room table. We used it only for Shabbat meals on Friday nights and Saturday noon. Otherwise we ate in the kitchen.

Father loved Mother so much. I remember it was her birthday or maybe their anniversary. We were at the dinner table. He came up behind her with his finger on his lips to tell us children to say nothing. He told Mother to close her eyes, then he put a sapphire pendant around her neck and kissed her.

It was one of the few things I managed to take away from Lodz after the war. I never take it off.

Our lives centered on family and synagogue. Mother was religious. On Fridays we celebrated the Sabbath with Mother lighting candles and saying prayers. Saturdays, Father and Motus went to the synagogue to pray. Mother, Bronya, and I stayed home: only men went to synagogue except for the high holidays and occasions, such as my brother's Bar Mitzvah when women would attend. We would sit with the women in the balcony. Only men sat downstairs.

Sometimes on Friday evenings, after our Sabbath dinner, father would give us money for the cinema. My mother didn't know this. Father said, "Tell your mother you're going to visit friends." He didn't want her to be upset that we sometimes broke the Sabbath.

I was a typical teenager: on Sundays, I loved to go ice-skating.

Weekdays I would skate at school where they had an ice rink. Weekends I would go to an artificial rink rather than a frozen pond in the park because I was afraid of water. I would take a couple of sandwiches in my pocket and skate from ten in the morning until evening. I loved going to the movies and collecting autographs from actors and actresses. I also collected butterflies, coins, stamps, and recipes that they taught us in school.

Like most Jews in Poland, Mother kept kosher. She didn't do much of the cooking or housework herself, because she was a businesswoman. She showed the maid how to prepare the different dishes for meat and dairy meals. For Passover, we had a completely different set of dishes. If by accident the maid used a milk knife for meat, it had to be buried in dirt for twenty-four hours. That was the Jewish law.

Bronya and I had a Hebrew teacher, Reichmann, a young man who came to teach us once a week. We played him up. When he arrived, the maid had his tea ready and so for half an hour we just talked. We didn't learn much Hebrew, just a few prayers. My brother went to a *heder* (religious school) after regular school, but my father eventually hired a private tutor for him. It was a great expense, but in one year he learned how to read, speak and pray in Hebrew. He also could translate all the prayers. At his Bar Mitzvah he did a beautiful job.

On that Saturday morning we all got dressed up and went to synagogue. Motus wore a new suit, made by our tailor, and a white shirt and tie. In synagogue he put on his *tallit*—the prayer shawl. Bronya and I wore new matching black velvet dresses with hand embroidery on the neck and bodice. Motus read from the Torah, and we were all so proud. After the service, we all went back to our apartment for a festive meal. Our whole family—uncles, aunts, cousins—was there. Our apartment was very crowded with over 40 people in attendance.

Mother did the catering with our maid. We had a traditional Sabbath meal—chicken soup with noodles, gefilte fish, roast chicken, potatoes, and a carrot *tzimmes* (carrots cooked with cinnamon, sugar and lemon juice). Seven years later, when we were starving to death in the slave labor camp at Salzwedel, Bronya had a dream. The next morning she told the girls in our barracks, "I had such a wonderful dream. It was Shabbat, and we were eating dinner: chicken soup with noodles, gefilte fish, roast chicken and *tzimmes*, the lot."

"You dreamt about all that food," one of the girls said, "and you didn't share it with your sister! How selfish can you be?" And we all laughed.

Motus' Bar Mitzvah picture
January 1937

Our family in Lodz. I would guess early summer, 1937: (from l to r);
myself 15, Bronya 17, Mother 37, Motus 13.

Antisemitism before the war

Like many other Lodz Jews, my parents, David and Lea, were in the textile business. With over 250,000[1] Jews, this textile center had the second largest Jewish population in Europe. One out of every three people in Lodz was Jewish.

Even before the Germans arrived there was plenty of antisemitism, but we tried to ignore it. My parents had built up a successful outerwear wholesale and retail business in Lodz, manufacturing suits, coats and school uniforms. They were resigned to stay. Seventy-five percent of our customers were non-Jewish Poles, Ukrainians and Germans. Just before the war, however, there was one incident that opened my father's eyes. This is what happened.

Mr. Szymansky, my parents' best customer, would always arrange his buying trips so that he would arrive at noon on Fridays because he knew that Mother was preparing the Sabbath meal. Although not Jewish, he loved her cooking, especially the festive Sabbath meal which was especially delicious. Mother would make sure it was fully prepared in time for Mr. Szymansky to come and sample it.

In January or February 1939, after the Christmas season, Father traveled as usual to some of the smaller towns around Lodz to collect money from some wholesale customers. He had never gone to Szymansky's store because he always paid his bills on time, every week like clockwork. This time, however, since he was near Kalisz where Mr. Szymansky's store was located, he decided to stop and visit.

Before entering the store, he crossed the street to get a better view of our merchandise displayed in Szymansky's store windows. There Father saw a beautiful display of our goods and a big sign that read, *Nie Kupoj Weroby Zydowskie* (Don't Buy Merchandise Made By Jews). Father was shocked — so this was the Szymansky who loved to eat Sabbath dinner at our house on Friday afternoons!

Father didn't go into the shop — he didn't want to embarrass Mr. Szymansky. But he knew it was time to leave. In an instant he realized what he had tried to deny for years: there was no future for his children in Poland. When he got home from Kalisz, he said to Mother, "We must go to America." He planned to go to the World's Fair in New York and fill out all the necessary papers. Unfortunately, by the time the World's Fair opened in New York, in May 1939, it was too late. Most Jews were trapped inside Poland.

Father at Ciechocinek Spa, early thirties

Father went every two years to a spa to drink the waters. He had stomach trouble because he kept all his worries inside him.

On the other years, we rented a cottage in the country. Everything was so fresh and green when it was hot in the city. Every morning we had fresh milk and eggs, and just-picked vegetables—radishes and scallions. Not lettuce. We thought lettuce was food for cows. Barbara and I wanted to go barefoot like the country children, but our feet were soft and white. Townies' feet.

My last picture of Mother and Father

I would guess that this was taken by a street photographer in February 1939. Winter, of course, because they're in winter coats. Father's was pure wool, lined with fur. Always he was well-dressed, Mother, too. She's wearing her Persian lamb coat. Always, she wore beautiful hats and shoes, and carried beautiful purses. It was part of her job as a business woman, but she loved good clothes. I do, too.

The Germans arrive

On September 1, 1939, German troops invaded Poland, marking the beginning of World War II. For the next three days they bombed the city. Then on September 8, the day I turned 17, the Germans occupied Lodz.[2] I remember watching lines and lines of soldiers, tanks and trucks moving down the street.[3] We were very frightened and bewildered.

The next day I went, as usual, to my evening class in accounting. All through school I had lots of friends, both Jewish and Gentile. Now, all of a sudden, my Christian friends shunned me, treating me as if I were a disease. Shocked and hurt, I ran home.

"Hannele, don't you know?" Mother asked. "Jewish children are no longer allowed to go to school." She always called me Hannele, it was her pet name for me. It was the beginning of the term and I had always loved school, especially mathematics, and hoped to become an accountant.

As soon as they gained control over the city, the Germans targeted Jews for special persecution. They came to our apartment building where over three hundred people lived. They ordered all the Jewish men to assemble in the courtyard. My father went down and joined the other men who were lined up.

Watching from our second floor window. I couldn't believe what I saw. Right there they beat the men and took them away. All day long, we didn't hear from Father —we had no idea where he was.

When he returned that evening, we didn't recognize him. Father, who had always been so neat and clean, always so well dressed in a suit and beautiful white shirt, was filthy, black and blue and swollen. After he washed, his face was a mass of bruises. He couldn't talk and he wouldn't talk.

Father had always been such a gentle man he wouldn't even kill a fly. "If God created a fly," he would say, "there must have been a reason. So why should I kill?" And now, just because he was a Jew, he was all beaten up.

In spite of the German occupation, we had hoped to stay in business. Our store was not visible from the street because it was located on the second floor as part of our apartment, but with a separate business entrance. We had many customers of German descent who had always been very respectful of our religion. They waited to shop in our store until after sunset on Saturday night when our Sabbath was over and we opened our doors. We had a reputation for excellent merchandise.

Once the Nazis took over, however, these same customers changed. I remember one incident in particular. A German family, good customers, came to our store and had their son try on a coat. They wore armbands with swastikas. After their son found a suitable coat, they asked for the price. My father quoted 32 zlotys. Smiling, they said, "Maybe you will take ten zlotys, or maybe five, or maybe nothing." Then they walked out with the coat. So much for our loyal customers.

Life under German occupation became unbearable. It was a nightmare. On November 14, they set fire to many synagogues in our city. That was how they commemorated the first anniversary of *Kristallnacht*, when they had destroyed over 1,000 synagogues in Germany and Austria.[4] I remember walking on Koscziuszko Street, around the corner from where I lived, and seeing the beautiful temple burning and burning. The firemen weren't allowed to put out the fire. We had to stand and watch.

Our family tried to run away with a neighbor and his family. Riding in their horse-driven wagon, we traveled to the countryside and found shelter with a local Jewish family. The house was very crowded, filled with many others who, like us, had sought refuge. The conditions were primitive: no beds, no food, and limited toilet facilities outside the house. All day long there was nothing to do except sit on the floor. After a few days our family returned home to face whatever there was to face. Others packed their belongings and traveled further east to Russia.

Life under the Nazis

Back in Lodz, we heard that the Nazis had gone to the hospitals and killed the sick people. Those who could ran away. It didn't matter if the patients were Jewish or Gentile, they were all killed. Later on we learned that the Germans had also killed the handicapped, the mentally retarded, and the blind. They killed Gypsies, too.

They made a law that we had to wear armbands, white and blue with a blue star to identify us as Jews. Later on the law changed and we had to wear a yellow star with *JUDE*, the German word for Jew, written on it. These stars had to be sewn securely on the front and back of our clothes so that we could be seen coming and going.[5] There also was a curfew — Jews had to be off the streets by 7 pm.[6] We weren't allowed to have radios anymore.[7] They had to be turned in to the authorities. Bronya and I brought our big *Telefunken* to city hall — it took the two of us to lift it. Naively, I asked the government official for a receipt. Smiling, he told us that he would send it by mail, but, of course, he never did.

Since Jews could no longer buy goods from non-Jewish shops, it was difficult to get groceries. The Jewish grocery had a very limited supply of food. At first, our Polish maid shopped for us in the non-Jewish stores. But soon we had to let her go because the Nazis made a law: Christians could no longer work for Jews. Not only was this a hardship for us, but also for our maid. She lost her job.

The violence escalated. Often, when Germans saw a Jewish man with a beard walking on the street, they would surround him and pull his beard, or cut it with scissors, or use a cigarette lighter and burn it. I remember those men screaming in pain. The soldiers stood around, laughing.

Whenever a soldier passed us on the sidewalk, we had to step down and walk in the street. We couldn't be on the same level as a German soldier. Sometimes, when we walked near the park, we would look up and see men hanging from trees. The Germans would be standing by, smiling. Whoever passed by had to stop and watch.

My uncle, Jacob Miller, Mother's brother, was arrested as a spy. The jail was in an area that had once housed a church complex. Now the Germans had taken it over. They called it the *Kripo*, short for Kriminal Polizei (criminal police).[8] Uncle Jacob wasn't a spy: he was just very outspoken. He liked to go to cafes and talk politics. In Europe at this time there was no free speech; people could not openly criticize the government. But my uncle read the paper every day and gave his opinion freely. Obviously he spoke to the wrong people, because when the Germans arrived, they arrested him.

Most days his wife visited him in jail and brought him some soup, but one day my mother went instead. When he came to the gate, she didn't recognize him. His face was all battered, his nose broken, his eyes so badly bruised he could hardly see. Only after he called out her name, "Lea, Lea," did she recognize him by his voice.

Every Thursday was called "Bloody Thursday" because they would beat the prisoners. Some died from their beatings, while others suffered through another week. Uncle Jacob was in that prison for two weeks. After the second Bloody Thursday, he disappeared and we never saw him again.

Another member of our family, my cousin Salek Borenstein, also died early on. He was from Radom, a nearby town in Poland, but by early 1939 he was studying engineering in France. That August he visited us in Lodz. He was very tall, very handsome. I was short. I took his arm as we walked in the street. People turned to look at us, and I was so proud.

Salek was with us when he got a telegram from his mother. He had to return to Radom immediately to join the Polish army. He was selected for the cavalry. He was killed in September, one of the early casualties. At least he died defending his country.

The rest of us were quite helpless. We were forced to submit to the Nazis and their proclamations. For over five years, more than thirty-six members of our family were trapped in Poland at the mercy of the Germans. Only my sister and I would survive.

Salek Borenstein, my cousin

"He died defending Poland."

Street hanging

In those months before we went to the ghetto, you would see people hanged in the street. They knew what they were doing. They were murdering innocent men. They enjoyed it. Look at their faces.

Aryanization

One day I glanced out the window and saw the Nazis enter our apartment courtyard. They marched into all Jewish businesses on the ground floor — the leather store, the clothing store and the grocery— and took away all their merchandise. I felt so sad for the store owners but relieved that our business had been spared. Attached as it was to our second floor apartment, it was invisible from the street. As the Nazis were leaving the courtyard, however, I noticed a Polish woman in a shawl, talking to an SS officer and pointing up at our apartment.

Not long afterwards the Gestapo banged on our door. They took everything away: the school uniforms, the suits, the coats, all our business equipment. On the way out, one soldier stooped down to pick up a button lying on the floor. Our store had been stripped bare, thanks to our Polish neighbor.

From September 1939 until we were sent to the ghetto in May 1940, there was no work for Jews. We were forced to live on our savings. Since the hours when Jews could shop were very limited, food was a problem. Luckily we had some distant cousins who owned a bakery. They lived quite a distance away, but at least we could visit them and get some bread. It was stale and frequently a little mildewed, but we ate it anyway. It helped fill our stomachs.

Before the war began, we children were all picky eaters. No matter what Mother said, we would eat very little. Now, with food in short supply, the three of us developed huge appetites. We became hungry teenagers who couldn't get enough to eat. Mother, who had a sense that things were going to get much worse, tried to save some extra food, but we always asked for second helpings.

In the middle of April 1940, we heard an announcement: all Jews had to move into a ghetto by the end of the month. It was located in an old, run-down section of Lodz, which formerly housed many Jewish families. As they became more prosperous, they moved to other sections of the city. Now all Jews were forced to return. Father hired a man with a horse and cart to help move some of our furniture to our new quarters in the ghetto.

Just before leaving, Mother gave me a corset to put on.

"Why do I have to wear a corset?" I asked her. "I'm so skinny."

"I have money hidden in the lining," she told me.

I felt it carefully. It seemed like a lot of money. I wore the corset when we moved into the ghetto, and then four years later, in August 1944, when the Nazis sent us to Auschwitz.

Father took a pair of Motus's shoes to the shoemaker who removed the bottoms of the heels and drilled out a space for Father to hide three large bills. After Father deposited the money, the shoemaker put the last layer back on the heels. Motus wore those shoes when we moved into the ghetto, and later when we were shipped to Auschwitz. Of course, once we arrived in Auschwitz, we had to strip naked, and the Germans took our clothes and shoes. The money didn't help any of us.

Another day right before we moved, Father and I were alone in our apartment. He gathered together all our remaining family wealth — jewelry, British pounds, silver kiddush cups — and placed everything on the kitchen table. He divided this treasure into three piles.

Taking a hammer and chisel, he removed the plaster from the wall and removed some bricks from under our windowsill. Into that space he shoved one-third of our goods, carefully replacing the bricks over them. I helped him replaster the wall, painting over it. He hid the other piles in two other places.

Father figured that whenever we needed money, we could return to our apartment, remove some valuables and exchange them for food. After the war when I returned to Lodz looking for my family, I tried to retrieve those items—but that's another story.

The ghetto is sealed

On May 1, 1940, the ghetto was completely sealed.[9] There was no longer any way we could leave and return to our apartment. We were totally cut off from all the valuables we had so carefully hidden.[10] A bungalow on Rawicka Street became our new living quarters. It had a kitchen, a small eating area and two bedrooms. Living with us was our father's uncle Anchel Szpilman who played the trumpet before the war. The house was small for the six of us, and the roof leaked — I remember not having enough buckets to catch the rain. But at least the family was together. Growing in the small yard were some weeds which we managed to cut down, chop up and cook. They gave us some extra nutrition.

A cellar with a dirt floor opened off our kitchen. In it we stored some of the potatoes that we managed to bring with us into the ghetto. Our maid had bought them for us. Mother had saved these potatoes for just such a time when we would have restricted amounts of food.

Uncle, who slept in the kitchen, would sometimes sneak into the cellar and steal a few potatoes in the middle of the night. At first we didn't notice anything missing. But soon we discovered that the potatoes were disappearing faster than we could eat them.

One day while walking to work, Father spotted Uncle exchanging some potatoes on the black market, trading them for cigarettes. Another time Father saw Uncle exchanging potatoes for a bowl of soup. Out of respect, he never confronted Uncle Anchel about his stealing. Nor did he tell anyone else. A short time later Uncle Anchel died. All his life he had suffered from high blood pressure. Only after his death did my father tell the story of the potatoes.

Soon the Nazis ordered us to move to another section of the ghetto, to a one-room apartment on Zytnia Street. This space was even smaller than our bungalow, and the little furniture we had brought with us could barely fit in. We had two twin beds and a small fold-up cot. Except for my brother, who slept on the cot, the rest of us slept in twos. Our small cooking stove kept us warm.

Fortunately, this apartment house had a little garden in back, which the residents had divided up into small beds. Each family grew beets, carrots, and other vegetables. Some people had brought seeds, which they shared with us. Every night a few people would keep watch over the garden to make sure no one stole anything.

Life was very hard, but we adapted. My parents taught us to accept our situation because we had no other choice. We focused on our Jewish traditions and tried to observe the Sabbath. Mother would light the candles and say the blessing. Even with the little food we had, she managed to make a Sabbath meal. She would take a bit of sugar and farina and mix it with an egg, salt and pepper. She would roll this mixture into balls, which she would place in a pot of boiling water with some carrots and onions. In this way we would have mock gefilte fish. Later on, when we ran out of sugar, she used saccharine. After a while, even that became impossible.

When we ran out of our extra provisions we had to make do with only the meager food we could purchase in the ghetto.[11] We were issued a book of coupons for the exact number of people in our family. These coupons allowed us to buy a few items — a quarter loaf of bread per person a week, a piece of meat the size of a hamburger, which was not beef, but horsemeat.[12] Occasionally we had an egg and a few vegetables. We never had any milk products, butter or sugar. Some people didn't even have enough money to pay for what they were allotted. They sold some of their ration coupons to buy food. What helped many of us get through the day was the watery soup they gave us at work, so at least our stomachs were a little full at lunchtime.

Even though the Nazis had confiscated our goods, we still hoped to do some business in the ghetto. The previous fall, right before the Nazis cleared out all the goods in our store, Father had cut up many large bolts of fabric into smaller bundles. These he gave to my mother's brother Moishe for safekeeping.

Moishe was one of Father's best tailors. He did the sewing from his house in Baluty with other tailors whom he employed. Although most tailors had only seasonal work, Father gave Moishe work year-round, providing him with bundles of material cut into patterns both before and after the season so he could have an income.

When the ghetto was established, Baluty, a poor area of Lodz, became part of it, so Uncle Moishe did not have to move. Once we were forced into the ghetto, Father approached Moishe and asked him for some fabric back so we could exchange it for food. Uncle Moishe refused. Even though Father had previously been very kind and fair to his brother-in-law, Uncle would not share any of the fabric my parents had given him. That is what hunger did to people, even family members.

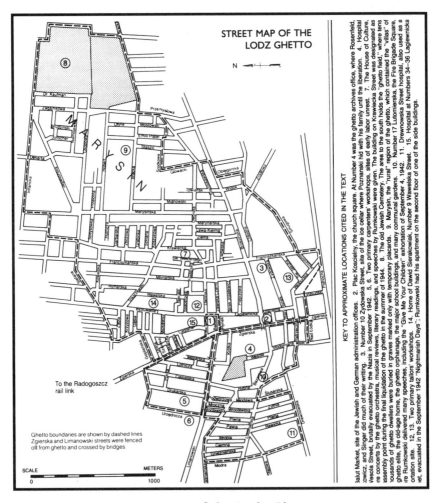

Street Map of the Lodz Ghetto.
Angie lived on Zytnia Street (see lower right-hand corner). Each day she walked over the bridge to labor at the straw shoe factory.

A boy kneels in doorway, his head resting on a soup pail. He dreams of soup.

Until death grabs him by the heels, the ordinary ghetto resident must travel a strange road.

Before death takes its victims from the world, it paints sorrowful pictures on their faces. Shadows of what once were called people walk the ghetto's streets, people with sunken, black, or grey cheeks, with eyes that glare like hungry wolves in the deepest woods during the coldest winters.

A person like this walks with eyes glaring, his breath feverish, his heart pressed down by an enormous weight, and his guts feeling like some beast was constantly gnawing at them.

Such a person does not "walk" but drags along like an accursed specter. When other people see him, their hearts stop. Those glaring eyes, they touch your intestines, and you realize suddenly: " I, too, am terribly hungry. Soon, I, too, will drag along with a glare in my eyes, breathing feverishly like him. "

Hundreds, thousands, drag along the ghetto streets now. They are driven from their houses into the streets, into the courtyards where garbage is piled, and they look, they seek:

A piece of broken pot that can still be licked—
A rag that once wrapped food and still be gnawed at-
A discarded piece of vegetable—
And they live out their last days up to their neck in piles of garbage.

Josef Zelkowicz, Sketches as quoted in
Lodz Ghetto, pp.128-129

Working in the ghetto

During those four years our family was very productive, working long hours, six days a week. Father was appointed to work in a tailor shop to inspect the clothes being produced for the Germans. They told him, "If you ever put anything in the crate that does not belong there, or that is not 100% perfect, we're going to kill you." In the morning when I kissed my father good-bye, I never knew if I would ever see him again. That's how it was in the ghetto: we were always frightened — all of us.

My mother and Bronya were sent to sort vegetables for use in the ghetto — potatoes, carrots, onions and turnips. They were not allowed to take anything home, but Bronya took a risk. She made a hole in the lining of her pocket where she could hide three to four potatoes that dropped to the bottom of her coat. I believe her supervisor knew what she was doing, but since she liked my sister, she turned a blind eye. After September 1942, Bronya was transferred from the food warehouse to work in a textile factory, and that was the end of that.

Motus worked in the ghetto's city hall, typing up lists of people for deportation. If Motus knew anyone on the list, he would take the names off —at the risk of his own life. At the time we didn't know about the death camps. We did know that once people were shipped away, they were not heard from again.

We had no news from the outside world; there was no mail, no radios, and only the ghetto newspaper, which had no news in it at all except who was going to be deported and how much food we were allotted. The news featured a story about someone who had stolen a piece of wood. We had no idea of gas chambers or crematoria. We were told that people were sent East to work on farms or in factories. Later on we began to suspect that they had been killed, but who could imagine the mass murder of hundreds of thousands of people?

I was appointed to work in a straw shoe factory making outer boots for the German soldiers who were going to fight on the Russian front. These boots would provide added insulation against the cold Russian climate and prevent frostbite. Another factory braided the straw, which they packed into bundles and distributed to us. Each of us had to produce four boots a day. Whoever did not meet this quota would lose her job and be shipped away. Our hands, unused to such work, got callused and bloody, from working with the long needles, twine and rough straw.

My parents had always raised us to be good and kind, not to stand by when people needed help, but to do something. On either side of me sat two girls who were too sick and weak to work. I remember them as if it were yesterday. One had straight, black shoulder-length hair with bangs. She had a beautiful face and skin, very fair against her dark hair. She wore a brace around her neck, which she quickly took off any time the foreman came by, so he would not see that she was sick. The other girl had short dirty blonde hair and an upturned nose. She didn't look Jewish. We weren't friends exactly. Neither girl had grown up in Lodz but had been sent to the ghetto from one of the small surrounding towns.

I knew that if at the end of the day those girls hadn't made their four boots, they would be killed. I was a fast worker and I helped them.

This is how I did it. Every morning when I came to work, I would first make two half-shoes, one for each of the girls. I left the needle sticking in the shoe so if the foreman came to check up on us, the girls could pretend to be working. Towards the end of the day I would finish their shoes. I made 12 shoes a day. It gave me a great deal of satisfaction to know that I had accomplished something. Helping these girls gave me more courage to live.

The straw shoe factory

It doesn't hurt to have an admirer

I was lucky, too. The man in charge of distributing the straw bundles liked me. I told him that I wanted to help the girls.

"Don't worry, Miss Angie," he said to me. "I'll help you."

Although most of the straw was tough and very hard to work with, he would select three bundles of the best straw he could find, not too soft so it would disintegrate and not too coarse.

He told me I didn't have to come downstairs to pick up the straw as the other girls had to do. He would deliver the straw to the room where I was working. Sure enough, every morning I found three good bundles of straw at my place. He had kept his promise. That's how I could make so many boots.

He sent me special food, too. At lunch each day we all had to stand in line in front of the factory canteen. Each of us had a special ration coupon which we exchanged for a can of thin, watery vegetable soup. We took our soup back to our work stations to eat. One day a young boy came to our room, asking for Miss Angie. He presented me with a pot of soup so thick I could stand my spoon up in it.

"You don't need to give me your coupon," he said. I was surprised.

"Why am I getting this special soup without coupons?" I asked.

"It is from the foreman who gives you straw," he said.

"I don't want it. Take it back," I said.

The other girls shook their heads. "You're crazy, Angie. You have an admirer who sends you good food and you refuse it. At least take it home for your family." But I did not want to be obligated to him.

"If I accept the soup without coupons," I said, "he'll want me to come up with a dessert, and I don't want that."

"Tell the foreman that if he'll accept my ration coupon, I will accept his soup," I said to the boy.

Soon the boy brought back the soup. With a smile he said, "The foreman will accept your coupon."

I ate some and took the rest home. To thicken it, I put a little flour in a frying pan, browned it and added water. The soup helped fill our stomachs.

One day while on my way back home from work, I saw the foreman walking with a lady. He excused himself and ran over to me.

"Marry me," he said. "Otherwise I am going to marry that lady. I am very lonely and don't want to live alone."

The proposal surprised me, but I turned him down. It's true he wasn't very goodlooking, but that wasn't it: I just didn't like him.

I wished him the best.

After he was married, he stopped giving me the special soup, but he never stopped providing me with the three bundles of good straw.

The administration of the ghetto

The ghetto was isolated from the rest of the city and the world. It had its own city hall, run by Jewish workers like my brother, and a Jewish police force, supervised by the Nazis. It even had its own ghetto money, which was worthless outside of the ghetto. Chaim Mordecai Rumkowski was the leader, or *älteste*, of the ghetto. He believed that as long as Jews were productive and useful to the Germans in their war effort, the ghetto would be allowed to exist. Maybe he wasn't altogether wrong, for the Lodz Ghetto was very productive: it remained in operation for four years, from May 1940 until August 1944. It was one of the last ghettos to be liquidated.

Survival in the ghetto came at a price. Rumkowski had to fill weekly quotas of those considered unproductive, mostly older people and children. Every week he had to ship away thousands to their deaths.

We hated Rumkowski. Before the war, he had been the director of an orphanage. Now he acted as if he were a king. He and his family never went hungry. They always had the best of the available food, wine and clothing. They were well fed and well dressed. Transported through the ghetto in a carriage pulled by a pony, he greeted the Nazi higher-ups as if he were one of them. He even tried to have stamps and money printed with his face on them, but the Nazis didn't allow it.

He thought he was indispensable to the Nazis, that he and his family would survive. He was mistaken. In August 1944, when the ghetto was liquidated, he and his family were deported to Auschwitz where they were all killed upon arrival.

Life in the ghetto

Each morning before we set out for work, Mother gave us some coffee and a little bread. It wasn't coffee: it was brown brew made of roasted beans and chicory, but at least it was hot.

It took me twenty minutes to walk to work. In my wooden shoes I had to cross a large wooden footbridge constructed over Zgierska Street that cut through the ghetto. Beneath the bridge Polish people rode the tram. For me the walk wasn't just physically exhausting, but mentally exhausting as well. In the summer when the windows were open, I could hear families fighting over food. Hunger had turned decent people into animals. Our family tried to share what there was and to give Father a little more. We accepted the situation. In order to survive, we had to accept that we would be hungry, and there was nothing we could do about it.

After work, Bronya and I tried to help mother by buying our food. Frequently, however, there were long lines. Even though it was quite late when we came from work, we needed to shop quickly and return before curfew began. By the time we reached the head of the line, little food remained available.

Most of us were starving. In the streets we sometimes had to step over the bodies of people who had died of starvation, wasted corpses with gray, shrunken faces. My parents told me that on the German death certificates the cause of death was never listed as malnutrition, but always pneumonia or heart attack. The Germans never told the truth. It was like our ghetto newspaper, which never reported real news. The worst was to see small, malnourished children, used as horses, pulling heavily laden carts—children who had lost their childhood.

Evenings we kept ourselves occupied. Bronya and Motus played cards, my parents played dominos and I knitted. Father had an old pair of Jaeger underwear made of very fine wool. Because he had frequent colds, Father had purchased several pairs for both winter and summer use. When they were new, the wool would help absorb the perspiration. Later in the ghetto, they wore out, with holes under the arms. I unraveled all the wool, pieced it together, and knitted myself a sweater, skirt and hat. The wool was off-white, an ugly grayish color. One week when we got some beets, I cooked them in a big pot of water. We ate the beets. Later I dipped my knitting into the juice. It gave me a pink outfit, which looked really good.

Once when I was standing in line to buy food, two men came to our one-room apartment and ordered my parents to hand over their fur coats. Jews could no longer have them. When we first moved into the ghetto, Mother had concealed hers underneath a specially made cloth coat. At least the fur kept her warm. Father's coat also had a fur lining, in the style of men's coats at that time. Shortly after Jews were prohibited from owning fur coats, my parents stopped wearing them altogether and kept them hidden. Then the police came to our house and searched till they found them. Someone had obviously betrayed them.

Neither of my parents would tell us what had happened. When I found out, I cried. They had worked so hard to be able to enjoy this luxury. It was the last of our valuables. Those warm coats had given them a little sense of security, and now they too were gone.

Bridge in Lodz Ghetto

Boys hauling cart

. . .I think the worst was to see small malnourished children, pulling heavily laden carts—children who had lost their childhood.

Angie Suss Paull

Gehsperre: September 5-12, 1942

In early September, a *gehsperre* (curfew) was announced. For seven days, from September 5-12, we were not allowed to leave our apartment until we were called out. They told us that they needed between fifteen and twenty thousand people, mostly children and old people, to be "resettled." That was a lie: they picked whomever they wanted. To be "resettled" was another lie: they were to be murdered. But we didn't know that. How could we?[13]

On September 7, our names were called. We had to leave our doors wide open so the authorities could make sure that no one was hiding. Where could anyone hide in our one-room apartment? Father, Mother, Bronya, Motus and I all went out dressed in our nicest clothes because we thought it might be a selection for jobs.

The soldiers told us to line up in front of them. To my right was a woman holding the hand of a little girl, maybe five or six years old, with a beautiful head of blond curly hair and blue eyes. She looked like Shirley Temple. A German officer grabbed the child, but the mother held her hand firmly and wouldn't let go.

"I don't need you; I only need her," the officer said, pointing to the girl.

"She is my child. I am going with her," the woman answered.

"You have thirty seconds to make up your mind," he snapped.

After a short time he asked, "Well, have you made up your mind?"

"Yes," she said. "I am going with my child."

"Turn around," the officer said.

He raised his rifle and gave a bullet first to the child and then to the mother. Instantly they fell to the ground.

We were next. The soldier grabbed my mother. I wouldn't let go of her hand; dead or alive, I wanted to be with my mother. But my luck was different. Instead of shooting me, the soldier just pushed me away with his rifle. That was my first miracle.

They marched Mother off with the other people selected for deportation. Some Jewish policemen guarded them. We just stood there, shocked. We all started to cry. One of the policemen, who knew my brother, asked, "Why are you crying?"

"They took my mother," Motus said.

Even the policeman was surprised. After all, the Germans claimed they were looking for old people. My mother wasn't old; she was 44.

"Let the soldiers leave," the Jewish policeman said to Motus. "I know where they're going. They're taking everyone to the empty hospital. Come with me. I'll find your mother."

Immediately Father ran back to our room and grabbed some warm clothes. He gave them to Motus.

"Go, Motus, go," he said.

Motus ran to the hospital with the policeman. They spotted Mother on the ground floor, standing right by the window. They could easily pull her out because the windows had no glass in them and there weren't any German guards around.

"We're safe," the policeman said. "I'll pull your mother out from the window."

She was almost halfway out when, from nowhere, a German soldier came and pushed her back inside. We never saw our Mother again.

Boy saying good-bye

"A grievous blow has struck the ghetto. They are asking us to give up the best we possess—the children and the elderly. I was unworthy of having a child of my own, so I gave the best years of my life to children. I've lived and breathed with children. I never imagined that I would be forced to deliver this sacrifice to the altar with my own hands. In my old age. I must stretch out my arms and beg: Brothers and sisters, hand them over to me. Fathers and mothers, give me your children!

". . . I must tell you a secret: they requested 24,000 victims, 3000 a day for eight days. I succeeded in reducing the number to 20,000, but only on the condition that these would be children below the age of ten. Children ten and older are safe. Since the children and the aged together equal only some 13,000 souls, the gap will have to be filled with the sick.

". . . I understand what it means to tear off a part of the body. Yesterday I begged on my knees, but it didn't work. From small villages with Jewish populations of seven to eight thousand, barely a thousand arrived here. So which is better? What do you want: that eighty to ninety thousand Jews remain, or, God forbid, that the whole population should be annihilated?

Excerpts from a speech by Chaim Rumkowski on
September 4, 1942 in *Lodz Ghetto*, pp. 328-331

September, 1942

**Jewish police catch Jews trying to flee through the
rear window of the ghetto hospital**

*By Januaury 1942 Jews held in this hospital would most likely be
deported to the Chelmno death camp, about 45 miles west of Lodz.
Chelmno was the first camp to use poison gas for mass murder. Jews were
killed by being loaded into mobile gas vans, trucks with sealed
compartments that served as gas chambers. By September 1942 over
70,000 Jews and 5,000 Roma met their deaths at Chelmno. Angie
believes this is how her mother died.*

No news

It took me over forty years to find out what happened to her. I learned that the Germans had taken the Lodz deportees to Chelmno, a death camp they had constructed. They drove the Jews there in trucks, which they had converted into mobile killing vans. On the journey, they pumped in carbon monoxide. On arrival, they removed the bodies and threw them into a big pit which they had prepared. They covered the bodies with dirt, dead or alive. My mother must have been one of them.[14]

I will never forget the last time I saw her on the afternoon of the selection, in that beautiful summer dress — bright flowers against a black background. Her hair was black—she hadn't a single gray hair on her head. She was only 44.

Father put on a brave face. "Don't worry, children," he told us. "Mother has just gone to work. She's very smart, she's brave: she'll find her way back." But every night I could hear him crying. He, who had always been so careful about his appearance, often forgot to shave. He just didn't care, so I would have to remind him.

I tried to take Mother's place, kissing him before he went to work, making a little fuss over him, giving him a bigger piece of bread, a larger portion of soup. But, of course, without Mother, life was just not the same anymore.

No news came into the ghetto. We didn't know about the German invasion of Russia in June 1941. We didn't know about Pearl Harbor or about America entering the war in December. We knew nothing about the siege of Stalingrad in 1943. Until we got to Auschwitz, we didn't know about the gas chambers and crematoria.

Now and then there were breaks

Day followed dreary day. We lived the best we could, hoping against hope that the war would end and life would return to normal. We were always hungry. One day Bronya came home with a bag of potato peelings. I washed them carefully to get all the sand out, and then I boiled them. While they were still hot, I mashed them with some coffee grounds, saccharine and a little water and baked it into a cake. Delicious? Well, to us who didn't have any sweets, it seemed so.

The cherry tomato

Once a month someone from the Judenrat (Jewish Council) would come around to see who needed extra nourishment. In truth, we all needed it, but one had to be lucky to be chosen. Those selected were invited to the ghetto kitchen for a special dinner. My sister Bronya was lucky—she always looked pale. Not me. Every time they came to examine us, I would turn pink in the face with excitement — I never looked sick enough. If I could have that special meal, my family could divide my portion that evening. Bronya, who was pale and didn't blush, was chosen several times.

For one of those meals, Bronya received a salad with a cherry tomato on top. She hated tomatoes and wouldn't eat one if her life depended on it. But she knew I liked them. In the dining room, Bronya could eat as much as she wanted, but when she left, she couldn't take any food out with her. They inspected everybody. What could Bronya do? Looking at the cherry tomato remaining on her plate, she had an idea; she popped it into her mouth and left. When she returned home, she washed it off and gave it to me. What a wonderful present!

Sixty years later in Rochester, New York, we both attended an elegant bridal shower, with pink tablecloths and napkins. The waiters brought us salads with cherry tomatoes. Barbara and I just looked at each other and smiled. We remembered.

The heart-shaped ring

September 8, 1943 was my twenty-first birthday. Father surprised me with a heart-shaped gold ring with my initials *A.S.* engraved on the outside, *Lodz 1943* on the inside.

"Where did you get such a gift?" I asked, astonished.

"It's nothing," he said. "I just exchanged it for some soup."

That ring was so precious to me. For weeks, perhaps months, Father had traded his soup for small pieces of gold, which he gave to an old friend, a jeweler, to make into the ring. And he was starving like the rest of us.

Motus gets pneumonia

In June 1944, Motus became ill with a high fever. It was pneumonia. He couldn't go to work, nor could anyone take him to the hospital where they might kill him. So Motus stayed home, too ill to move. I wanted to go home and feed him a little.

Everyone who worked in the straw shoe factory was given a special pass once a week for one hour. We could go on errands or go home. We had to leave our ID card with the guard at the door. One hour gave me just enough time to visit Motus, for it took me twenty minutes to cross the bridge and walk home, twenty minutes to be with Motus, and another twenty to return to the factory. At least I could check up on him and give him hot soup and some words of encouragement. Each time I walked though the door, he told me, it was as if I brought the sunshine.

Now something wonderful happened. Since I had been good to those two girls in the factory, helping them produce their daily quota of boots, a few others girls gave me their weekly passes so I could visit Motus every day. There was only one problem. I had to remember my new name for the day. I had to leave the ID card at the door. If I forgot my name for that day when I returned, not only would they kill me, but also the girl who had given me her ID card. But when your life is at stake, you remember.

Every day Motus got a little better. Whenever I came, he would be writing in a notebook, which he would let me read. He wrote about our family, the way we lived before the war, and what had happened to us in the ghetto. In it he poured out all his feelings, about how cruelly we were treated, about how we had lost Mother. I had no idea how much sadness he had kept inside. He expressed himself so beautifully that I brought his diary with me when we went to Auschwitz. But, like everything else, it was taken away.

The liquidation of the ghetto

Liquidation of the Ghetto

On August 8, 1944, Motus received a letter to report August 10 for deportation. "You're not going," I told Motus. "You're not strong enough. I'll go in your place. The Germans don't know Polish names: it doesn't matter if a boy or girl shows up, as long as they have a person to send away."

"No, I'm going," Motus replied. "I'm feeling better and I won't let you take my place."

I don't know which one of us would have won that argument, but everything changed. In the middle of the night the Jewish police came running from house to house shouting, "Tomorrow is the liquidation of the ghetto. Tomorrow is the liquidation of the ghetto." There was no choice; now we all had to leave.[15]

That night we prepared our bags. Not knowing where we were going, but thinking we might be going to work, we packed whatever we could stuff into our knapsacks. We didn't have much anyway. I put in some clothes, my autograph album, my stamp collection, and a book of recipes I'd collected when I was in school. I also grabbed Motus's diary.

The next day we left the ghetto. Although it was hot, we dressed in layers of warm clothing. Maybe they would send us to Siberia. While we were standing outside our door ready to leave, Father handed us a piece of paper. On it were the addresses of our aunts, uncles and cousins who lived in the United States.

Then he said, "Children, listen. We don't know where we are going, who will live, who will die. Whoever survives should go to our family in the United States. Maybe we will meet again."

Suddenly Father said, "Go back inside. Don't look."

Usually I listened to my father, but this time I disobeyed and I wish I hadn't, for what I saw will remain with me until the day I die. Across the street I saw German soldiers taking little babies from their mothers' arms or pulling them out of baby carriages. Grabbing them by the legs, the soldiers threw them against the wall and then onto waiting trucks, like pieces of garbage. All this they did with a smile. Babies! They didn't want to waste a bullet on the babies. This I can never forget.

Father, Motus, Bronya and I assembled outside the building. The Nazis marched us to the train station where cattle cars were waiting. They laid down boards and we climbed in. We were packed like herrings so tightly we couldn't move. To sit or lie down was impossible. People were crying and screaming. There was one bucket for over 80 of us to use as a toilet. It quickly became full to overflowing. The stench was unbearable. It became terribly hot and when people fainted, there was no room to move. The crowd held them upright.

I have no recollection of how long I was on the train. There was no food or even water. It seemed to take forever. We lost all sense of time.

We had no chance to say "good-bye"

Finally the train came to a stop. The guards opened the door. We had arrived at Auschwitz. We saw German shepherds and soldiers running around yelling, "*Schnell, schnell, schnell!* —fast, fast, fast! Leave all your baggage on the train."

They herded us out of the cattle cars and assembled us on the platform. We marched through a gate with an inscription on it that read *Arbeit Macht Frei*— work makes you free. For a moment we were happy. "Good," we thought, "we're going to work." But very soon we knew it was a lie. There was the terrible stench from the chimneys; we wondered what was burning.

The men were immediately separated from the women. That was the last time I saw Father and Motus. We had no time to say good-bye. For years, I kept on asking about them, looking for their faces in photographs. In America, I would watch World War II documentaries on television. My sons would ask, "Haven't you had enough of the war?" I couldn't tell them I was looking for the faces of my family, hoping that they had somehow survived and found their way to America, as Father had told us to do.

There was no closure on these deaths. After more than sixty years, there's no closure now.

Father had actually been one of eight hundred men selected to remain behind and clean up the Lodz Ghetto, but he wanted to be with his children. Had he agreed to separate from us he would have survived. The Germans had intended to murder them once they had completed their work, but the Russians liberated the area, and the men were saved.[16]

Deportation to Auschwitz, August, 1944

5,000 a day were sent from Lodz to Auschwitz.

Arbeit Macht Frei
Entrance to Auschwitz

"I've no idea how long the journey took. I lost all sense of time. When we arrived, the doors were slid open and the Germans were screaming, 'Schnell, schnell, schnell.' On the entrance gate to the camp were the words 'Arbeit Macht Frei' (works makes free). 'Good,' we thought. 'They've brought us here to work.' But it was a lie. Then the men were separated from the women. That was the last time I saw my father and brother. We had no time even to say good-bye." **Angie**

What happened to Bronya and me

We left our luggage behind on the platform. We were marched to a large building. They ordered us to put all our money and jewelry into some large crates. All I had left was the heart-shaped ring my father had given me. I was not going to let the Germans have it. I quickly took it off and buried it in the dirt with my heel.

Before we entered the building, a female guard spied Bronya and told her to take off her shoes. They were hand-made and beautiful. The guard took the shoes and left Bronya standing in her bare feet.

As we entered a huge empty room, they told us to take off all our clothes. We had to undress and stand naked in front of the soldiers. Who had time to think about our dignity? Everything was *schnell, schnell* — fast, fast.

They marched us into an empty hall. We had to sit on barrels turned upside down where Jewish barbers, also forced into slave labor, shaved us under our arms and wherever we had hair. Most girls were completely bald. I looked around and couldn't find my sister.

"Bronya, Bronya." I called out.

"I'm here," she said. "I am standing right beside you."

She no longer had her beautiful, wavy, baby-fine brown hair. She looked like a monkey. Not wanting to hurt her feelings, I said, "Oh, I didn't see you."

All of a sudden, the other girls started throwing bobby pins at me. I didn't know why. Touching my head, I felt that I still had a little hair. It had always been so thick and coarse, like a brillo pad. Perhaps the barbers were afraid of blunting their clippers. They did not cut it all off, but they left me with a boy's haircut. I really didn't want to have hair — to look different from all the others.

I caught three bobby pins, which I still have to this day.

They gave us soap and a towel and ordered us to line up, still naked, before the open doors of two huge shower rooms. I was in the middle of the line; Bronya stood behind me. The guards pushed all the girls in front of me into the first shower room and closed the door. We waited and waited for what seemed a long time. The second shower room remained completely empty. Finally, they switched us to the other shower. Later on we realized that the first shower room must have been a gas chamber. If they had taken one more girl, I would have been killed.

To this day I don't know why they switched our line. Maybe they had too many bodies to get rid of; maybe the machinery malfunctioned. In any case, we had real showers with water. That was my second miracle.

As we left the shower room, they gave us each a dress — no underclothes, no shoes, just a dress. Some girls managed to get wooden shoes, but the rest of us remained barefoot. They marched us to a large barracks with a sign over the door, Number 26. Inside were rows and rows of bunk beds in three tiers. There were no mattresses, no blankets, just wooden boards. The barracks had been emptied, awaiting our arrival. Later on we found out that Gypsies had lived there before our transport arrived. Maybe they were gassed to make room for us. We feared that we might be next.

We filed in. Five of us had to sleep in one bunk. Bronya and I shared a bunk on the first level with three other girls we had never met before. The five of us were squeezed in so tightly, just like sardines, that every time one of us turned, we all had to turn. There was just no room to move. Nonetheless, we fell asleep, exhausted.

The next morning, a comb fell on Bronya from one of the upper bunks. She handed it to me.

"Oh, I've lost my comb," exclaimed one of the girls in the top bunk.

We said nothing. After all, she had no hair to comb, and I did.

A guard came in, yelling. "Get up. *Shnell, raus*, quickly get out."

We went outside. It was our first roll call. They made us stand in rows and started counting us. We stood still until they were satisfied that everyone was accounted for. Then they gave us a coffee-like drink, brown water made of chicory, and a slice of black bread. We had to return to our barracks. There was nothing to do, just walk around or sit on our bunk beds. We couldn't leave. Some of the girls were so weak that they just went back to bed.

The days were very long. The only time we could leave our barracks was for roll call. They counted us constantly; day or night, it didn't matter. The days were endless and all the time we were scared. They warned us if anyone was missing, we would all be punished.

And toilet detail. There was a shed with maybe one hundred and fifty holes, side by side. We couldn't go to the bathroom when we wanted, only when they wanted. And they gave us maybe three minutes. Since many suffered from diarrhea, there were many accidents. We had no toilet paper, no place to wash our hands. How could we clean ourselves?

We had to wear the same dress all the time, day and night. It was August and the weather was unbearably hot. After a few days we needed to wash our dresses because they smelled. We went into the washroom, where there were sinks and washed them with the cold water. We put them back on, letting our body heat dry out the dresses.

Interior of women's barracks in Auschwitz-Birkenau

This photo, depicting the squalid, crowded conditions of life in the concentration camp, was taken shortly after liberation. It appeared in the poster exhibit Auschwitz: A Crime Against Humanity *which came to Rochester in 1987. After overhearing a visitor trying to imagine what it must been like to sleep there, Angie spoke up to reveal that she knew. For 40 years she had been silenced by the disinterest of others. Now for the first time she discovered herself sharing her painful experience with others who wanted to know and learn. This marked the beginning of Angie's outreach and educational mission.*

Latrines at Auschwitz

"There was a shed with maybe 150 holes. Of course, there was no toilet paper. There was no water to wash our hands. How could we keep clean?"

Angie Suss Paull

Food at Auschwitz

We had to stand five in a row to get some soup and a piece of bread. The first girl got a can of soup. She passed it on to the next in line. All five of us drank from the same can. If you were lucky, you got a piece of potato or turnip to swallow. If not, maybe tomorrow would be your lucky day. The best place for the bread was in your stomach. If you saved a little for later, somebody would grab it.

Once, one of the girls rummaged through a pile of garbage and found a rotten carrot. The German guard caught her and took her back to our barracks. We all had to follow. She had to pull up her dress and bend over. He took out his whip and gave her twenty-five lashes on her bare behind. She screamed in pain. Imagine, giving twenty-five lashes to a starving girl for taking a rotten carrot from a garbage pile! He told us that if any of us commit the same crime, we would get the same treatment.

Not long afterward, this same girl found another carrot and again was beaten. This time, she didn't cry. She had no more tears.

There were many other occasions when guards beat us with their whips. They struck us if we did not move quickly enough. Most of the time they beat us for no reason at all. It all depended on their moods.

I was lucky; I was never beaten. Being short, I managed to hide between taller girls. I was afraid of that first beating. My sister was beaten just once, in her face, for no reason.

I wasn't the only one with hair. Another girl who stood right in front of me at roll call had a full head of hair. She was beautiful, even in Auschwitz, with long, soft, wavy hair and a curvy figure. She had more clothes than we did. Over her dress she would sometimes wear a sweater. She didn't look as if she were starving either. Though the German guards were forbidden to associate with the prisoners, someone was obviously looking after her. Sometime later she disappeared. Rumor had it that a guard had raped her and killed her so he wouldn't be found out.

The white cloth

After that first night when we saw the flames from the chimneys, we knew about the ovens and what they were burning — the bodies they killed in the gas chambers. What we had smelled when we arrived was human flesh. We lived in constant dread of being killed. We also feared being deported. Who knew where we would be sent?

Besides the fear was the boredom, long days sitting in our barracks with nothing to do. We hoped we would be selected to do something, anything. The days were so long.

On the morning of our tenth day in Auschwitz, we had another roll call, but this one was different. They ordered us to take off our dresses and come out naked. We feared the worst had come, that we were going to be killed. We saw doctors in white coats standing there and making selections. They checked out each girl. Anyone who looked sick, anyone with a blemish or a scratch, was selected to go to the gas chamber.

I was especially nervous because that morning Bronya had awakened with a nasty pimple under the left side of her nose. We had always tried to look clean. Now she had a pimple filled with puss. Holding my hands with palms together I looked up at the sky. In my heart I begged God, "How can I save my sister?"

At that moment I looked up at the sky and saw a little cloth flying down towards me, a beautiful piece of white cloth, maybe 4 x 4 inches in diameter. It was so pure I did not know where it had come from.

I grabbed it and quickly wiped my sister's pimple. I waited, holding onto the piece of cloth, until right before the doctor walked by to inspect us. Then I wiped the pimple again and threw away the cloth. This time I squeezed it until it turned white.

We both passed! This was my third miracle.

Transport to Bergen-Belsen

Immediately after, we boarded the waiting trains. Again they shoved us into cattle cars. We had no idea where we were going. More terrible nights and days, no room to sit or lie down: no food, no water, and one overflowing bucket for all of us. I remember the smell, the packed bodies, the heat, the hunger, and the thirst.

Even so, I was lucky. I was jammed in against the side of the cattle car. A missing slat created an opening about eight inches high and two feet wide. I had a little air to breathe! When the train came to a halt at one station, a young soldier on guard at the platform looked in, saw my face and threw me a piece of bread through the opening. Why did he feed me? Was it because I had some hair and looked a little more human? Who knows? I did not get the bread, however. Some other girls behind me snatched it and ate it immediately.

At another station, the guards divided our train. Some of the cattle cars were unlinked. A third of us stayed on the main train. Our car was the last one to remain connected. It took us three days and nights to reach our destination. We were the lucky ones. The girls on the other cars traveled for four more days before they reached Bergen-Belsen. They had no food, no water. When they came to our tent, they fell onto the floor, exhausted.

Bergen-Belsen

Our arrival at Bergen-Belsen was the same as at Auschwitz, guards running around screaming, "*Schnell, schnell,* fast, fast!" We were marched to a huge tent, which was empty except for the straw covering the ground. We had no blankets, but it was the end of August and still warm. We still wore the dresses they had given us at Auschwitz, and we were still in our bare feet.

The food was also the same as at Auschwitz — coffee-colored water, a slice of dry black bread and a thin soup. This time, however, we had individual cans so my soup for the day was my soup. I did not have to share it with anybody.

September arrived: the weeks passed slowly. We were still tense, but not as tense as we were in Auschwitz where the flames of the chimneys and the smell always reminded us that we might be next. In Bergen-Belsen we didn't see any chimneys or gas chambers. But still they counted us constantly.

Aside from these roll calls, there was nothing to do; time dragged.

"How long can this go on? How long will the war last?" Bronya and I wondered.

"We just don't know," we told each other. We had to accept the war's dragging on and on—we had no choice. We had to accept hunger, accept filth, accept the everlasting roll calls.

In spite of everything, we never lost hope. Eventually the war would come to an end, we assured ourselves, and we would be reunited with our family. Always inside me I heard a voice telling me, "You'll pull through." In the straw shoe factory, in Auschwitz, and now in Bergen-Belsen, it kept telling me, "You'll pull through."

The days started to get very cold, gloomy, and rainy. At night, we clung to each other to keep warm. We lived one day at a time. We knew nothing of the outside world. We didn't even know that there were other areas in Bergen-Belsen where men were imprisoned, or that any Jewish men were still alive.[17]

A special holy day

One day some girls who worked in the kitchen returned to our tent and told us that Yom Kippur, the Day of Atonement and the holiest day in the Jewish year, would begin that night at sunset. We all remembered how we observed Yom Kippur with our families, fasting and praying for twenty-four hours.

That night, as the darkness of evening fell, we grew quiet in our tent. One of the girls began chanting the *Kol Nidre* prayer, that marks the beginning of Yom Kippur. She had a beautiful voice. Someone else took up the melody, and then another and another until the whole tent was full of that prayer. One of the guards, hearing our chanting, came into our tent and stood there listening. We kept on singing. The guard walked out, without saying a word. We were amazed. Even though religious services were strictly forbidden, this guard had allowed us to continue saying our prayers.

The next day we all wanted to fast. When they gave us our soup, we hid it in the straw. Later that afternoon right before roll call we broke our fast and drank our cold soup. It comforted us that at least for this one day we had affirmed ourselves as Jews.

Yom Kippur was a very special day, a memorable day amongst many grey, endless days.

Sometimes in our tent, Bronya would burrow in the straw to see if anything was buried there. Once she found a little mirror. She went to one of the kitchen workers and bartered it for a piece of bread. She quickly ran back to me, smiling with excitement, and showed me the prize. We split the bread immediately.

Deportation to Salzwedel

After six weeks in Bergen-Belsen, with roll calls day and night, we had a roll call that was different. The guards gathered together our same group of fifteen hundred girls, some Polish, some Hungarian, that had been selected at Auschwitz. They told us that we were going to be deported to work. We felt great. At last we would have something to do so we wouldn't think about food all the time and the days wouldn't be so long. At least we could be useful.

They ordered us to take showers. They gave us a towel and soap. When we finished our shower, we received a bundle of clean used clothes containing panties, a slip, a dress and shoes. They made no attempt to sort these items by size. Some tall girls were given short dresses while mine was very long. Instead of a slip, I got a long pink nightgown with lapels. My dress was dark green with long sleeves and a low neckline.

I decided to make myself an outfit. I put the nightgown on and then the panties, and stuffed the long bottom of my nightgown into the panties. Then I put on the dress, placing the collar of my nightgown on top of the dress. I didn't have a mirror, but I could see that it looked rather nice. Bronya received a different dress, a two-toned blue. The dresses were all different, probably taken from other prisoners and cleaned up. But it felt good to have fresh clean clothes. They also gave us blue-and-white-stripped coats. Mine was much too long for me.

We were taken to the cattle cars. I don't remember how long we traveled, but when the train came to a sudden stop, we jerked forward. Bronya fell onto the dirty rough wooden floor. She scraped her ankle; it was all bloody. When we walked off the train, the guard told us to report to the ambulance standing at the station. I was not allowed to enter with Bronya so I waited for her outside. Looking in the window I could see that the nurse did not clean the wound; she just put some black salve on it and bandaged it up. They told her to stay in the ambulance overnight. Bronya was delighted. She was going to sleep for once in a bed. But I was uneasy.

I overheard some nurses talking. Tomorrow everyone staying in that

61

ambulance would be shipped away, they said. When the nurses left, I banged on the window until I caught Bronya's attention and motioned for her to come out.

She opened the door. "What's the matter?" she asked.

"Come out at once,"

"Why should I leave? I have a nice bed inside. It's warm and comfortable,"

"Leave right now," I said. "I'll explain later."

Bronya came out and we got back onto the cattle car. Sure enough, the next morning everyone on the ambulance was gone. That was my fourth miracle.

They mark us as prisoners

The next day, after a short ride on the cattle car, we arrived at a labor camp in Salzwedel, Germany.[18] The whole camp, newly built, had a pleasing smell of fresh wood. We were ordered to go immediately to Barrack Number 4. Waiting for us at the door was Marysia. She was a very large young woman from Czechoslovakia, about 25-30 years old. Very tall, she weighed well over 300 pounds. She spoke German fluently and seemed on very friendly terms with the German guards. Marysia was our *Blochälteste,* the woman in charge of our barracks. It was divided into rooms each holding two-tiered bunk beds. We were happy to discover that we each had a bed of our own. The barracks were clean, and we were warned to keep it that way.

Marysia divided us up, eight to a room. Bronya and I shared a bunk bed. I slept on the top, she was on the bottom. In our room we also had two long wooden benches and a table. Each girl got a soup bowl and a spoon. It gave us such a lift. The menu didn't change, but at least we could eat again like humans.

The next day the guards brought us needles, scissors and pieces of thread. We had to rip off the left sleeves of our dresses, exchange them with other girls, and sew them back on. Bronya and I exchanged sleeves so that now my green dress had one long green sleeve and a shorter blue one. Over our dresses we wore blue and white striped coats.

While I still had the needle and scissors, I got an idea. If I shortened my coat, which was too long on me anyway, I would have enough material to make myself a hat. Always handy with a needle and thread, I cut 10-12 inches off the bottom of the coat. Folding the material in half, I made an eight-inch seam and draped the remaining material around me like a shawl. The other girls copied me, and we all had hats to protect ourselves from the cold weather that would certainly come. Even the tall girls decided to sacrifice some material from the bottoms of their coats so they could also have hats.

Marisa's assistant brought out a can of yellow paint and a brush. She painted two wide yellow stripes down the front of our dresses and a big yellow "X" in back. Now if anyone tried to run away, she would be recognized immediately as a prisoner. It made no sense to us. Where could we run? The perimeter of the camp was surrounded by barbed wire, which was electrified: anyone touching it would be electrocuted immediately.

Besides, why would we want to run away? We were able to work and have a reasonable place to stay. Conditions were cleaner here than at any of the other camps.

To mark us further, we were each given a numbered piece of cloth an inch and a half by four inches. My number was 8841; Bronya's was 8840. We had to sew these numbers onto the left front sides of our dresses. No longer could we call each other by our names, but only by our numbers.

After we had finished our sewing, Marysia chose two girls to go to the kitchen and get the barrels of soup. When we filed out into the hallway, Marysia ladled out our soup. We returned to eat the soup at the tables in our room. The soup was watery as usual, but it had a few more vegetables in it. After all the portions were ladled out, Marysia would call us back room by room for another half portion until all the soup was gone. Those who did not receive seconds that day would be first in line for an extra portion the next. My stomach was no longer used to eating that much at one time so whenever I was given an extra portion, I would have to put the soup aside for an hour or so. I couldn't wait too long, however, because I might suddenly be called out for roll call or another girl might take the soup when I wasn't looking.

One good meal

On our first Sunday in Salzwedel we took our turns, as usual, at the soup line. We were delighted to find bread and butter and a thicker soup than usual. It even had little pieces of meat in it. We were so happy.

"Could we be getting better food from now on?" we wondered. No such luck. The guards had thought they would give us this extra food to impress the Germans who were coming to inspect conditions at the camp. These officials were not pleased, however, to see how well we were being treated.

"If the prisoners receive food like this every day," they remarked, "they will get lazy and won't be able to work."

After that we went back to our normal near-starvation diet. As far as I can remember, during the seven months we were at Salzwedel, we had only one good meal.

The ammunition factory

Every morning after we had some substitute coffee and a slice of bread, we would file out for roll call. Then we were marched a short distance to the ammunition factory. All together there were some 1500 girls working various jobs. Bronya and I were among a group of 19 girls assigned to produce bullets. We worked in the corner of a huge factory floor where there were nineteen bullet machines. In a half hour we had to learn how to operate the machines. We were not allowed to ask any questions; just listen and obey. When the foreman finished his demonstration, everyone went right to work, everyone, that is, except me. When I turned on my machine, nothing happened. It was a lemon.

I was so frightened I didn't know what to do. I was afraid to go to the foreman. If I told him I couldn't operate my machine, he might ship me away. But how could I operate my machine? All of a sudden I spotted a huge ice pick in the corner of the room. It was very heavy; it probably weighed more than me. Somehow I managed to drag it over to my machine and place it between the spokes of the wheel that drove the machine. I jumped on the ice pick, using the entire weight of my body for leverage. Thank God, the machine started, but it took all my strength. And I had the same problem every time I filled up a crate with bullets. I had to stop the machine, have the crate removed, then drag over the ice pick to start the machine all over again. This happened several times a day. I became so exhausted jumping on the ice pick that I could hardly breathe or talk.

As I continued to work, I found myself getting weaker and weaker. After a few weeks I was spitting up blood. It became harder and harder to start the machine. For the first time I gave up on my life. I just couldn't go on.

That evening I told Bronya, "Tomorrow morning I am going to the foreman. I will tell him all the problems I am having with my machine. Either he will fix it, which will be fine, or he will have me killed, which will be better. That was the only time I gave up on my life.

Bronya started to cry.

"Don't cry," I said. "This is my choice. I can't go on like this any longer."

The next morning as I started to go to the foreman, the door opened suddenly and in walked three German soldiers in black uniforms. I walked back to my machine. The soldiers looked over all nineteen girls and stopped at me. They motioned for me to come closer. I stood up straight and declared, "My name is 8841."

One of the officers pointed to a table where three German ladies were sitting inspecting the bullets. He ordered me to leave my machine and join them. Again my life was saved. I didn't have to go to the foreman.

Before I could join the other women at the table, one of the soldiers gave me a gadget and showed me how to inspect the bullets. I had to grab some bullets as they were filling the crate and wipe the grease off with a piece of cloth. Then I had to check the bullets with my gadget. They shouldn't be too long, too short, too thick, too thin or scratched. If any of those five things were wrong, I should stop the machine immediately and call on Fritz, the mechanic. I was very happy to have this job. It was so much easier than jumping on an ice pick all day long.

One day while I was sitting at the control desk, the German lady next to me told me her story. She was raised as a Catholic and had married a member of the Nazi party. She had no idea that her grandmother was Jewish until she was arrested and sent to Salzwedel. I know she stayed in a different part of the camp from us, in better living quarters. Her husband would give the other two ladies at the desk food for his wife. Once in a while, she would share a thin piece of her sandwich with me. It was usually spread with lard. I don't know why she told me her story or shared her sandwich with me. Did she feel sorry for me? Or was she trying to bribe me not to tell anyone else about her Jewish grandmother? If so, she needn't have worried. I had other things on my mind than to snitch on her.

Back in the barracks, I washed out the rag I had used to check the bullets, put a little lard on it from the sandwich I was given, and rubbed it on Bronya's cattle-car wound. We shared the bread that was left. I repeated the treatment when I could. Because of the lard, the wound grew less dry and cracked, but it still didn't heal.

"It's not going to get better till the war is over," Bronya said.

I smacked her face. "Don't say that ever again," I scolded.

I don't know why I hit my sister. I just felt that once she said something like that, it would come true. Sure enough, the wound didn't heal until the day we were liberated.

Sabotage

One day while I was sitting at the control desk, the other ladies took a break for lunch and left me alone to inspect the bullets. I suddenly saw that some bullets were scratched.

"Stop the machine," I told the girl.

I ran to Fritz and showed him the bullets.

"It's the machine," I said. "It's *kaput*."

He looked around to see if anyone else was around. There were no Germans.

"Do you know whom these bullets are for?" he asked.

"Yes," I answered, "for my brothers and sisters."

"I hate the war," he told me. "I hate what Hitler is doing, killing innocent people. I'm going to show you how to sabotage the bullets.

"When you find defective bullets, let the machine run till the crate is three-quarters full. Then tell the girl to stop the machine. Call out loudly, 'Fritz, the machine is *kaput*' so the three ladies at the control desk will think what a conscientious worker you are. I'll come and fix the machine so there will be good bullets on top. The bullets are heavy, and it is unlikely that anyone will dig down to the middle or the bottom of the crate to inspect the bullets."

I don't know why I agreed to sabotage the bullets with Fritz. Why was I willing to take such a chance? Perhaps Fritz was testing me and would turn me in to the authorities. If so, I would be shot. But I trusted Fritz. He was about forty years old, short and bald with bowlegs. He had a good face, gentle. He would often be in trouble with the authorities. I would hear the foreman hollering at him, threatening to send him to Siberia.

From then on, for at least four months, Fritz and I sabotaged the bullets. We risked our lives. It got to be so routine that I hardly thought about it. I didn't say a word, not even to Bronya. But every time the French prisoners took away another crate full of defective bullets, my eyes would meet Fritz's as if to say, "Mission accomplished."

Conditions at Salzwedel

At Salzwedel we all worked two different shifts, six days a week. One week I worked days and the other week nights. It was very hard to adjust to these different schedules. When we worked days, we thought we could at least sleep through the night, but that wasn't to be. Every two or three hours they woke us up for roll call. Then we returned, exhausted, to our barracks trying to get some more rest. At least Bronya and I remained together on the same shifts.

In our spare time we were kept very busy. We had to clean our own barracks and maintain another that housed our toilet facilities. Without basic necessities, like toilet paper, soap, and toothbrushes, and without being able to shower, we were still expected to keep clean. At work we could not go to the bathroom when we needed to, but only when they wanted us to. Like in Auschwitz, the toilets were in rows and there was no privacy. They would march a group of us in and we had just a few minutes to do what we needed to do.

Living on starvation rations, we were always hungry. One day a girl from our barracks went into the kitchen area and searched through the garbage barrels looking for food. She found a rotten carrot. One of the guards caught her. He shaved her hair, which had just started to grow back, and stood her on a podium. On her shirt was a sign, "I stole a carrot." Everyone from our barracks had to walk around her and look while she stood for hours, holding a heavy bucket of water in each hand. We were sorry for her, but we couldn't do anything to help her.

At the end of March 1945, 1500 women from Theresienstadt came to our camp, filthy, covered with lice, and half dead. The guards squeezed them into the other barracks, but luckily not ours. These women didn't work. We wondered why they were in our camp, but we had no interest in seeing them. We couldn't help them. It's terrible to say, but we didn't want them in our barracks; we didn't want their lice.

Meanwhile the defective bullets started coming back from the front. They started to investigate who was at the control desk. I was scared to death. I knew it wouldn't be long before they questioned Fritz and me.

Waiting to be liberated

Suddenly everything changed. On April 12, 1945, we returned as usual to our barracks after we ended our shift at the factory. We found no lights, no water, no barrels of soup. We were puzzled. On the other side of the barbed wire surrounding our camp, a few Frenchmen were standing around talking to some girls. These prisoners lived in a separate camp. Their job was to load our crates of bullets onto the trains.

"Hold on," they said. "We did this to save you."

Soon we heard the details of what happened. One of the Frenchmen went to the German headquarters and overheard the officer in charge of the camp speaking to his men telling them that he had just received a telephone call from Berlin. He had an order to take the girls to the barbed wire and electrocute them. He was told that the American army is eight miles away and in two days they will liberate the camp. The officials in Berlin didn't want to leave any witnesses.

The officer told his men that he would not fulfill the order. " I am old and have had a good life. Let those young girls have a good life too."

The Frenchman ran back to his camp and told the others what he had just overheard. They were still concerned about the girls. They trusted the commandant, but not those working under him. One of the soldiers might still try to fulfill the orders and electrocute the girls. They decided to go to the main cable and cut off all the electricity.

For two days we had no food except for some sliced dried potatoes. There was no way to cook these few rations and very little water. The German cook came around with a barrel of water on a wagon. When he ladled it out, he purposely shook his hand so that some of the water would spill back into the barrel. All we got was half a cup. He did this out of meanness.

The next morning, all the Germans had gone—the controllers, the foreman, the guards, the German ladies at the control desk—all had disappeared, including Fritz. I never saw him again.

Liberation

When the American army entered the camp on April 14, 1945 they were amazed to find some girls still alive. Ours was the first camp they liberated where they found girls who were not dead or half-dead. The first girl they saw got a watch from a soldier. We were all overjoyed to see the Americans.

The German cook tried to run away.

"Stop." The American soldiers called out to him.

He kept on running. A soldier shot him in the back. He died instantly, falling forward on his stomach. We walked around the body, happy to see that this mean man had received his just reward.

An American officer told us, "You have two to three hours. Go out and do whatever you want to the Germans."

Weak from hunger, we thought about food, not revenge. We did not want to be the same barbarians as the Germans. Many girls ran to the bakeries for food and to the stores for clothes. The Frenchmen invited us to eat from the barrels of soup they had prepared for us. The Americans gave us boxes of food as well.

I get sick

We were liberated but I was not able to go anywhere. My whole body hurt. Curled up in pain, my stomach ached so much I couldn't eat. It was my first attack of what turned out to be gallstones. When we got to America, I nearly died from them.

One of my friends, a girl of about 16, stayed behind to look after me. Everyone else left the barracks and went out looking for food. Not being used to anything but a starvation diet, they all overate. Only my friend and I didn't get sick from overeating.

After my pain subsided, Bronya returned, bringing me some bread and soup. She also was in great pain from overeating, but, thank God, she recovered. The next morning she awoke, jumped out of bed and shouted, "Look at my leg. It's healed." Her prophecy had come true. Her leg hadn't healed until the war ended.

Bronya had also been able to find some clothes. She brought me a navy blue silky dress and a doctor's white coat. I cut down the coat and made myself a blouse. From the dress I made a jumper. I had to wash it. Not having an iron I waited until the dress dried. Then I put the jumper and blouse underneath me to iron out while I slept.

Some soldiers who spoke Yiddish came and interviewed us. I spent a few hours speaking to them. I don't know what they did with my testimony. I have never seen it.

Getting used to normal life

After years of starvation, our stomachs had to get used to digesting normal food again. For five years we had not eaten any meat, milk, sugar, butter or oil. Like invalids, we had to begin eating gradually a very light diet. It took weeks till we were able to eat normally.

We had to relearn other things that we used to take for granted — how to use toilet paper, a knife and fork, a toothbrush and toothpaste. Remember, we hadn't had toilet paper or brushed our teeth for years. The Germans had reduced us to animals; now we had to become human again.

After a few days, the American soldiers burned down our wooden barracks and moved us into the German officers' quarters, brick buildings with bathrooms and showers. They gave us soap, towels and toilet paper. Now we could take hot showers.

Soon men started coming into our camp looking for surviving family members. Some girls found a brother, some a cousin, others a father or an uncle. We were happy for them, but sad for us. Where was our family? Perhaps we should return to Lodz to see if any of our family had survived.

Exploring

We remained in Salzwedel for a short time until we got back our strength. During the day we would explore the countryside, making side trips to some small surrounding towns. As survivors we could ride the local buses and trains for free. One day we walked into a small town. We had no money so all we could do was window shop. As we were admiring some shoes in a store window we spotted a familiar-looking woman standing next to us. She had been a Nazi guard at Salzwedel; she had been very mean, constantly screaming at us and hitting us. Immediately we ran to the police station and had her arrested. British army officers were now in charge of the station.

"What should we do with her?" they asked.

"Why don't you cut her hair off," I said, "as they did to us in Auschwitz?"

"We don't have any scissors here," a policeman answered.

" I have scissors," I said, giving him the small scissors I was carrying.

"You cut it," he told me.

"No, I don't want to cut it; I want *you* to do it," I said.

Some of the other girls volunteered. And what a haircut they gave her, all uneven with part of her scalp showing. The Nazi woman didn't say a word, and we had the satisfaction of seeing her humiliated as we had been.

Return to Lodz

As soon as we felt strong enough, we began our return trip to Lodz. With no money, no passports or papers, we traveled by foot and train. At night we stayed in houses abandoned by Germans who had fled the advancing Allied army. We would help ourselves to food the panicked owners had left behind. One house we stayed in must have been a restaurant or a pottery store because we found hundreds of dishes in the attic and basement. After we ate, instead of washing the dirty dishes, we just threw them out the window into the backyard. After all, there were hundreds more. In another house we found a huge cheesecake. In the middle of the night we woke up so hungry we ate the whole thing.

We traveled on trains as war refugees, often running into Russian liberators. One Russian soldier was especially kind to me. His wife's name was also Andzia and I reminded him of her. He smiled at me and gave me a hug.

Another Russian soldier was not so kind. He blocked my path and motioned for me to come with him with a pail of water and brush. I was scared.

"I just came out of a concentration camp," I said.

"It doesn't matter," he said.

Luckily a young Jewish man stepped forward and shouted, "Leave my wife alone." The soldier ran away. I never saw my rescuer again, but I was so grateful to him.

We hitchhiked on trains; no one asked us for tickets. When we arrived at the train stations, officials would sometimes give us food and places to stay over night.

It took us three weeks of traveling. We joined a whole crowd of young people, all from Lodz. We were like family. An older woman, Edzia became part of our group and tried to protect us. She had been married and had a child before the war. Bronya and I called her *Mamushka*, the Polish word for mother.

When we finally reached Lodz, Edzia took Bronya and me to a Jewish friend's apartment. This woman had been married to a Polish gentile and, as far as she knew, had remained in Poland. Not knowing if she had survived, Edzia knocked on her door. The door opened, and, yes, she was alive. They hugged each other tightly and burst out crying. She was happy to give us all a room.

Bronya went to the building where the Jewish Relief Committee had established a Jewish Center. There they kept a big bulletin board listing the names of all who were alive. While Bronya searched in vain for any family names, I took my friend Heniek directly to our old apartment. I knocked on the door. A Polish man answered and I introduced myself.

"We lived here before the war," I said. "I'm looking to see if anyone from my family survived."

"You mean to tell me that Hitler still left some Jews alive!" he exclaimed.

"Don't worry," I answered. "I haven't come back here to live or to take away any of our furniture. That you can keep. I came to see if anyone from my family has been looking for me. Has anyone come? My father, my brother, my mother?"

"No, no one was here," he said.

At that moment I realized what I had dreaded all these years—that no family member had survived except for Bronya and me.

"I have some things hidden here," I said. "If you allow me to remove them, I'll reward you with something."

His eyes opened wide as if he were sitting on a gold mine and didn't know it.

"Can you give me a hammer and chisel?" I asked. He readily agreed.

I went to the windowsill and removed some plaster and bricks. I took out two kiddush cups and some jewelry and put them on a table behind me. The man started to grab.

"Why are you taking my things?" I asked. "I told you I would reward you with something."

"If I can't take whatever I want, I'm going to kill you," he said. He put his hand in his pocket and pointed something at me—I don't know if he really had a gun or if he was just pretending.

Heniek and I didn't wait to find out. We scooped up everything we could off the kitchen table and ran out the door. We managed to grab the kiddish cups, two men's gold pocket watches, some bracelets, Grandmother's 22-caret gold chain, and Mother's necklace with the sapphire pendant, which I wear to this day. I remember the love with which Father gave it to her on their anniversary.

As for the items hidden in the two other places, they are still there, unless the present owners have remodeled the apartment and found them. Let them remain hidden. After the greeting I received, I'll never go back to Poland again. Never.

Good-bye to Lodz

We spent two weeks in Lodz, talking to people who had returned from the camps, trying to find any information we could on the fate of our family. Eyewitnesses told me that Father had gone straight to the gas chamber. My brother Motus was killed three days later.

Edzia also had a terrible experience. She went back to the apartment where she had once lived with her husband and son and found no one. It was completely empty. She found a photograph of her child lying in a corner of the living room floor. Did the thieves leave that on purpose, to give her more pain? They had left nothing else, not even a scrap of paper.

When Edzia returned to us, she lit a candle in her son's memory. She never heard from her husband or son again. She never found out what became of them. It was time to leave: Poland was nothing but a graveyard.

From Lodz to the American zone

Edzia, Bronya, and I traveled together and met up with another group of young boys and girls returning to Germany. The journey from Salzwedel to Lodz had taken us about three weeks. Our journey from Lodz back to Germany took almost three months. By now the liberating forces had established control over the area. It was divided up into four zones: the British, French, Russian, and US zones. These zones were strictly patrolled. Anyone entering or leaving a zone had to show a passport or other identification papers. We had neither, so we had to cross borders illegally.

Along the way we met some Jewish officials who advised us on how to travel. "Avoid talking in front of government officials," they said. " Tell anyone who asks you that you're Greeks."

We traveled like hoboes, jumping onto any train going in the right direction. At night we scavenged for food and slept in empty houses or barns or even fields. From Lodz we had to cross the Russian zone and travel to Poznan. When we were in the Poznan train station, a Russian soldier came over to me. Because I was young with large dark brown eyes and dark hair, he thought I was a gypsy. He watched me waiting for the train with our group.

"Tonight you are going to tell me my fortune," he said.

I was very scared because I knew he wanted to rape me. *Mamushka* tried to protect me. The train finally arrived. Russian army officers boarded the train and made themselves comfortable in a first-class compartment. We seated ourselves in regular seats. Edzia, who spoke Russian, took me to the officers' compartment and knocked on their door.

" I have a young girl here who is very frightened. A soldier wants to rape her tonight."

"Let her come in," they told Edzia.

I will never forget how nice they were to me.

"Don't worry, don't be frightened," they said. " We'll protect you."

Two of the four officers stood up. One took off his coat, rolled it up, and made a pillow. The other removed his coat, told me to lie down, and covered me with it. I was still shaking. They took down two pieces of luggage from the overhead rack and made seats for themselves.

"Now," they said, "we need you to point out the soldier who is bothering you."

Sure enough, when the soldiers started boarding the train, I spotted him. The two officers left the compartment. I don't know what they did to him, but when they returned, they rubbed their hands together and said, "He won't bother you again."

I had a good night's sleep on the bed the officers made me from their bench.

Crossing borders

The following morning we left the train and continued on our way by foot until we reached the border of the Russian Zone. We had to get through the guard. One of the group, a woman, who was a little older than us, had a bottle of vodka. She used it to bribe the guard so he would let us through. She told him we would be coming through that night.

When we arrived we discovered that the guard had changed. We had no more vodka. What could we do? "Don't worry," she said. "I'll flirt with him while you smuggle through."

She had relations with him while the rest of us went through. He didn't know we were there. That's how she saved us.

Now we needed to get to the British zone. We had to climb up a steep hill. Out of the corner of my eye I could see a river flowing far below. I began to lose my footing. With nothing to hold on to, I didn't know how I could save myself. Suddenly, a boy behind me put his boot down, stopping me from sliding. I didn't even know his name, but he saved my life. Soon we reached the top and went down the other side of the hill.

When we finally reached the British zone, a British soldier came out of the guardhouse and pointed his gun at us, asking us for identification. Of course, we had none so we had to go back. The following day, we went through the woods, and this time we were able to pass into the British zone without being detected. Once there, a representative from the Jewish community found us, gave us papers, and told us to proceed to the American zone where we would be taken care of.

When we entered the U.S. zone, some officials put us on a train for Landsberg-am-lech, a displaced persons (DP) camp.[19] When we arrived there, however, we were told we could only stay a few days because the camp had become overcrowded. They promised to help us find a place in another DP camp.

At Landsberg we became like a big family, boys and girls living together in the same room. Evenings, before bedtime, we would put up blankets on a rope across the room to create separate sleeping quarters for boys and girls. Sometimes the boys would stand up and peek over the blankets to spy on us girls. We all shared the same bathroom.

One night, as I was coming out of the bathroom, a man approached me and asked, "Have you seen my watch?"

"What watch?" I said. "I saw no watch."

Perhaps he thought I had found his watch and kept it.

That evening I saw him again. This time he was carrying a box he had received from the Jewish Relief Committee. He told us his name was Jacob Suss. Before the war he had owned a carpentry shop. He had joined a group of people at the DP camp who had trades, such as carpentry, tailoring, shoemaking, plumbing, electrical work and baking. Some were musicians. They all volunteered to teach their skills to the survivors whose schooling was interrupted by the war. With new skills, these survivors would have an easier time getting jobs in their new countries and wouldn't be a burden to the government.

The volunteers had special privileges. They ate in separate canteens where their meals were served to them. We had to stand in line. They received special packages of food from the Jewish Relief Committee. Many people exchanged them on the black market for watches, jewelry and clothing. But Jacob was different. He shared his treasure with us. He opened the box and offered us the canned goods, coffee, jam and cookies.

"*Ess, kinderlach* — eat children," he said, smiling. He knew how hungry we were.

The next day I was scrubbing the wooden table in our barracks with sand. There was no soap. I spread the sand on the table, poured water on it, scrubbed it with a brush, and rinsed it off with clean water and a rag. It worked

Jacob Suss walked by.

"You like scrubbing?" he asked.

"No, as a matter of fact, I don't like it, " I admitted, "but I don't like eating on a dirty table."

Again he smiled.

Our first date

That evening Jacob asked me to go for a walk. We just walked around the barracks talking. Black cats ran around us. People said that it was bad luck, but I didn't believe it. We started talking about our families. At this time we still didn't know for sure what had become of them.

Jacob's family had lived in Dombrova-Tarnowska, a small town in southern Poland located between Cracow and Tarnow. When the Germans took over the town, the Jews were no longer allowed to pray in their synagogue or practice their religion. The men would pray anyway, using private homes. They would gather in groups of ten for a *minyon* or prayer group. One day the Germans discovered Jacob's father's group and killed them all while they were praying.

Someone ran to Jacob, who was working, to tell him his father had been shot. Jacob ran quickly to the house and saw his father wrapped, in his prayer shawl, holding a prayer book in his hand. At first Jacob thought his father was only sleeping as he sometimes did when he prayed. But when Jacob moved closer, he saw that a bullet had gone right through his father's glasses.

When the Germans began deporting Jews from the town, a Polish Catholic friend hid Jacob's brother, his wife and two children. The Pole made a false wall between two rooms in his house. When the Germans searched the house for Jews, they couldn't find anyone, but a German shepherd sniffed them out and all four of them were shot. Luckily the Polish rescuers were not at home or they would have been shot as well.

Jacob hid his mother and his brother's two children in his basement. That brother had escaped to Palestine before the war and had left his mother to care for the children. Some Poles became suspicious and told the Germans. They came to the house, searched the basement and discovered Jacob's family members. The Germans took all three out in front of the house and shot them. Jacob had to stand and watch, but he himself was spared because, as the Germans told him, they liked him a lot. He was such a good carpenter, they said, that he would be the last Jew in Dombrova to be killed.

Eventually the Germans decided to deport every Jew from the town. By this time Jacob was married and had a 22-month old son. They lined up all the Jews in the town square and herded them into waiting trucks. Suddenly, a German official called, "Jacob Suss, Jacob Suss, step out. We need you to work for us."

They told him he could choose ten assistants.

He picked his wife and nine other people, including a few women to be polishers. His wife came out holding the baby.

"Why are you bringing the baby?" the Germans asked. "We don't want the baby. You must leave him behind."

"No," Jacob's wife said. "It's my *baby*. He has to stay with me."

She wouldn't let go of the baby. The German officials shoved them both onto the truck. That was the last time Jacob saw either one.

Jacob did not have the heart to fill his wife's place, so he had only nine assistants.

It wasn't until after we married that Jake told me the details about his wife and child. I said to him, "If you want to tell me all about it to ease your pain, you may." But he never could.

All nine of Jacob's workers survived. When we were living in United States after the war, everyone came to our New York apartment to thank Jacob for saving their lives.

Jacob Suss proposes

Jacob and I had two or three more dates. With no money and nowhere to go, we just walked around the barracks in Landsberg and talked. After a few days, they sent our group to another DP camp in Felderfing, Germany. At first I heard nothing from Jacob. After a couple of weeks, he came to our room carrying an attaché case.

"Why are you here?" I asked, happy to see him.

"I came to see you," he said. "Miss Andzia, will you marry me?"

I wasn't really surprised.

"*Tak*," I said in Polish — yes. I had known that man only six days, but I had seen the goodness in him, how he had always cared for others.

"I knew you would say that," he said, and we both started to laugh.

He opened his attaché case and took out a piece of cooked brisket, cookies, and a bottle of vodka.

"Call the others in to join us," he said, "and we'll have a party."

They all came around.

"I'm getting married," I announced to the group. "Jacob Suss and I are getting married!"

Everyone wanted to give us presents, but they didn't have anything. So they brought us what they could. One came with a bar of chocolate, another with a smile, and so on.

Jacob pulled out a bottle of vodka. Everyone gave us congratulations and drank to our health. I really didn't know anything about drinking. In Lodz I was too young. All I ever had was some wine on the Sabbath. The vodka looked like water. I didn't know that each time you were just supposed to take a little sip. I thought I had to drink with everybody who congratulated me. So I had one drink, then another and another. After a while I started to giggle and couldn't stop. For the first and last time in my life I was drunk.

Soon Jacob had to return to his job in Landsberg. At that time there was no mail delivery from one camp to another. So whenever he found someone going to Felderfing, he would send me a love letter. They were wonderful. I wish I had kept those letters, but in all our travels, they got lost. In the letters he asked for the measurement of one leg, then for a sleeve, and then for the width of my waist. I couldn't figure out what he was up to.

He wanted to surprise me with some clothes. And he did. He ordered me a blouse, a suit, and a beautiful pair of boots, which at that time were very much in style. I was the best-dressed woman in the DP camp. I also had beautiful hats. I loved hats.

Angie in her new suit and hat

The double wedding

It was September 1945. My sister Bronya had became engaged too. Her fiancé was Herman Mondrowicz. We knew his family before the war. They owned a shoe business where we used to shop. It was located on the same street where we and they lived. The Mondrowicz's were a big family and very religious. Herman's brother was a Hasidic Jew, very learned. Bronya met Herman when he joined our group traveling together from Lodz to the US Zone in Germany. Herman's brother also survived the war and moved to Palestine. He remained very religious.

On March 24, 1946, we had a double wedding, Bronya and Herman, Jacob and I. It was held in the ballroom of the Hotel Schwann on Klingenstrasse 15, in Marktredwitz, Bavaria, a region in Germany. The Hotel had been turned into a temporary hostel where we survivors lived after we left Felderfing.

Bronya and I both had beautiful wedding dresses made from white satin that Jacob gave us. Jacob also found a Hungarian Rabbi from a nearby town who agreed to marry us.

Jacob was what we called "an organizer." He knew how to get things done. He got a hold of a typewriter on the black market and then went to the director of a cloth factory.

"You want a typewriter?" he asked.

Of course, the answer was yes. Typewriters were very difficult to come by. In exchange, the director gave him the white satin.

Then Jacob went to a dressmaker and gave her coffee to make the dresses.

For the wedding cake, Jacob went to the American officers' dining hall.

"We're having a double wedding. Could you help us with some ingredients?" he asked.

They gave him a sack of flour, sugar, butter, and two cases of champagne. All this he took back to the Hotel Schwann. Jacob had to guard this treasure carefully so it wouldn't be stolen. He took the flour, sugar and butter to a bakery and had 10 cakes made.

The wedding was held on a Saturday evening. We had lots of people — at least 150 people attended, mostly survivors that we had met in the DP camps. Jacob organized everything. He rented dishes and we did all the cooking. We made our own ice cream with a machine he was able to rent. Jacob even found an orchestra to play live music — tangos, waltzes, polkas and fox trots. All the men lined up to dance with me. It was a joyous celebration.

Double wedding: dresses

*On my wedding day I cried. Why? I remembered complaining to my
mother before the war that I never got new dresses of my own, I always
got the clothes Bronya had outgrown.*

*"Would you like to be married on the same day as your sister?"
Mother asked. That's how it happened. My mother's voice came to me.
Yes, I did get married on the same day as Bronya, and so I had to have a
new dress of my own.*

Wedding ceremony

Life in Marktredwitz

Some people told us that our room at the Hotel Schwann used to be Hitler's office during the war. After that Jacob would lean out the window smiling, and say, "Heil Hitler," and he would make the Hitler salute. Jake was a *kibbitzer*. He loved making fun, telling jokes and stories.

In Marktredwitz, Jacob organized a synagogue in the ballroom of the Hotel Schwann. We had services on the Sabbath and Jewish holidays. He also organized soccer games.

Saturday nights he would hire a live band for dances in our hotel ballroom. On special occasions, we would cook a delicious meal and set the tables beautifully with dishes and silverware rented for the occasion. Everything sparkled on a beautiful white tablecloth. We invited the officers and some dignitaries from the American unit in town to join us. Jacob saw to it that I had beautiful clothes, a new dress for each dance. Everyone had a wonderful time.

But I was not entirely well. In the middle of the parties, I would frequently have to retreat to my room and lie on the bed, curled up like a lizard. I continued to have attacks of the terrible pain in my stomach that started in Salzwedel the day we were liberated. The pain was unbelievable. It went through my body, my stomach, my belly and up my back. Sometimes I would have three attacks in one day. When the pains passed, I got up, washed, made up my face, and went back to the dance. I acted as if everything was normal.

When I went to the doctor, he took x-rays, but nothing showed up. He gave me pills for my liver and B-12 injections three times a week to build up my body. But the attacks continued.

The doctor in Marktredwicz had no idea what was wrong; he guessed it was nerves. He suggested that I get pregnant. He felt that a baby would take my mind off the past and give me a future to look forward to. By September, I became pregnant with David. He was born June 2, 1947, six months before we sailed to America on the USS Marine Flasher. And, yes, for nine months the pain stopped. But when we were living in New York City, it came back. Something had to be done: I couldn't avoid pain by getting pregnant all the time.

Three years later, after we had moved to New York City, I finally had to have surgery. By the time they opened me up, they found an infected appendix and gallstones the size of walnuts, which they removed. They also cut the nerve from my stomach to the gall bladder. After two weeks I was still in tremendous pain and was almost dying. The surgeon came to my house; he couldn't believe I was in so much pain. He had tears in his eyes. He thought for a moment and then touched some nerves in my back near my ribs. I screamed.

"I think we're saved," he said,

He rushed me to the hospital, took a long needle and blocked four more nerves in my back. The pain finally stopped and didn't return.

Angie's ID Card in Marktredwitz, Germany
Issued in April 1946

Marktredwitz, Germany April 1946

*We commemorate our first Holocaust Remembrance
Day with a parade. Bronya and I are in the in the
front row with the wreath between us. Bronya,
wearing a scarf, is on the right and I am on the left
with the big hat and boots as was the fashion at that
time.*

Jacob Suss, Marktredwitz, Germany, 1946

To Jake Suss (7 years old) from Grandma, Rochester, 2001. "This is your grandpa, Jacob Suss (the man with the smile). He was very athletic: he played football, coached it, and refereed it. His usual place was left back, and I remember him scoring a goal. When you played, you were left back, and you, Jake Suss, scored a goal. Wasn't that a coincidence?"

How we got to the United States

Every time we registered after the war, we always stated that we had family living in the United States, but did not know their addresses. Meanwhile Uncle Izzy had a friend in the US Army who was going to be stationed in Berlin. Izzy asked this friend to look on the list of survivors from Lodz to see if his brother David Szpilman or any of his family survived the war. Through this friend, Izzy found out that Bronya and I were still alive and began working on papers to bring us to the United States. By that time, Bronya was already engaged to Herman, and I to Jacob. After we were married and I had the baby, they had to redo the paperwork. David had to be at least three months old before we could arrange for our physicals and prepare other legal papers. Bronya and Herman left before us.

December 12, 1947: God Bless America

Finally we were able to leave Germany. We sailed on the Marine Flasher, a United States warship during the war that was converted to a transport, taking survivors, amongst others, to the United States. Men were housed separately from women and children. Although I needed his help, Jacob was not even allowed to see the baby. In addition, I found myself caring for another baby whose mother had became paralyzed. The doctors came to examine her and find out why she had no feeling in her legs. Meanwhile Jacob became so seasick he came to me for help. I hid him on and off in our cabin with the paralyzed woman and child. I looked after all of them.

Waiting for us at the pier was my Uncle Sam Szpilman who brought us back to his apartment for dinner. I was so happy to see his wife Shirley and their daughter Gery whom I had known before the war. Jake met them for the first time. We were so grateful to them and also to my Uncle Izzy who had signed the affidavits of support, the guarantees that had made it possible for us to come to the United States. As gifts we had brought them beautiful dishes and figurines we had purchased in Germany.

Soon we were reunited with my sister and Herman who had sailed to America two weeks previously. They had already changed their names. Bronya became Barbara and Mondrowicz was shortened to Mand. The Szpilmans had managed to find an apartment in their building for Barbara, Herman, Jacob, David and me to share. It was small for four adults and a baby, but we were lucky to have it. With the soldiers returning home after the war, apartments in New York were difficult to find. With just two rooms and a kitchen, it was still far better than the one-room apartment five of us shared when we were herded into the Lodz ghetto. So we managed. Our American family bought us all new furniture. "After what you've gone through," they remarked, "we don't want you to have to sleep on other people's discarded beds."

Nonetheless our new beds were so crowded together in one room that when Herman, who had found a job in a bakery, left for work in the middle of the night, he had to walk over our bed.

Jacob finds a job

We arrived in New York on a Friday, December 12, 1947. Right away Jacob, who now became Jake, started looking for a temple. Someone told him that on 12th Street there was a congregation whose members came from Dombrova.

The next morning, he left for Sabbath services at the 12th Street Temple. He was excited at the possibility of meeting people from his home town. When the service was over, a Mr. Goldstein came up to him and said, "Jacob Suss, in Dumbrova, when I was hungry, your father gave me bread. Now it's my turn to give you bread. I have a job for you. Come to my office on Monday."

"Thank you," Jake said, "but I'll start on Tuesday."

"Why not Monday?" Goldstein asked. "You have a family and need a job."

"Thank you," Jacob said, " but I will come on Tuesday. Tuesday is a lucky day for me."

The next day, Sunday, two ladies from the Temple sisterhood came to our apartment. One of them had been the Suss's next door neighbor in Dombrova. Jacob knew her very well. They started telling stories about their hometown, talking about who had survived and who was gone.

"We know you have just arrived and have no money," she said to Jake. "You have a young family. Here is some money to start your life." She handed him a thick envelope, 9" x 12".

He looked at her and said, "Thank you very much, but no thank you. I cannot accept your money. I want to start off my new life with my own two hands."

When they left, I told Jake how proud I was of him.

"Angie I have a feeling I'll make a good living in the United States," he said. "Besides, I don't want anyone pointing a finger at me, saying that they gave me the money to start my life. I don't want to feel obligated to anyone."

On Tuesday, December 16, Jacob went off to work for Mr. Goldstein. Meanwhile, I got to work on our apartment. The first thing I did was scrub the floor. The room was so small that to scrub it I had to move the bed next to the door first one way and then the other. I managed. Each night I had to pull the bed down from the wall and each morning put it back up again. My knuckles got bloody.

By that first evening, the place was clean, and I had a hot meal ready for us.

Friday, Jake got his first paycheck. He borrowed a dime for the streetcar from one of the workers and handed me the envelope unopened. "On our wedding night, I opened your envelope," he said. "This time it's your turn."

He was paid a small salary, but we thought ourselves rich. Why? I was translating dollars into Deutsche marks. I thought, "Soon we'll be able to buy Rockefeller Plaza."

It wasn't much money, but still we saved. I was very careful: I did all our washing myself rather than spend money on a laundromat. Every week, I put money aside. And every week, we sent a parcel to Germany to Jake's brother Joseph who was still in Marktredwitz in the Swann Hotel. In it were cigarettes, coffee, and clothes.

My visit to the Jewish theatre

My Aunt Shirley took me to the Jewish theatre around the corner from where I lived. Performing there was a comedian named Leon Fuchs, a tall, thin man with a long neck and an Adam's apple. He made jokes about the government: he was so funny everyone was laughing. Everyone except me. I was crying.

"Why are you crying?" my aunt asked. "This is meant to be funny."

I remembered my uncle, Jankel Miller, who had been arrested as a spy and killed for talking politics. I remembered the years of being too terrified to say anything against the government. I remembered all the time in Auschwitz, in Bergen-Belsen, in Salzwedel, never being able to speak out, never being able to complain.

"I'm crying," I said, "because in Poland you could never make jokes about the government. Here in America I know I'm free. I'm crying because I'm so happy."

Jake learns formica

Jacob was always very good with his hands. He was also good at languages — before he came to America he spoke Polish, Yiddish, German, Ukrainian and Russian. When we lived in New York, he went to night school to learn English and math. He wanted to learn how to convert measurements from the metric system we used in Europe to the American system of feet and inches.

His boss, Mr. Goldstein, wasn't a carpenter, but a contractor. Jake worked under a Ukrainian carpenter who wouldn't tell Jake the secret of how he glued formica to make countertops. Jake couldn't figure out the trick, that the glue had to be attached to the wood at just the right time so it would stick properly. Always when the Ukrainian was about to bond the formica to the counter, he would send Jake on an errand — to the wholesaler for supplies, to the post office, or to the coffee shop for coffee.

This went on for a month: Jake couldn't learn the secret of Formica, so he developed a plan. One morning he came in to work early. He made a small hole in the door between the bathroom and the workshop. Then he nailed calendars over the hole on both sides of the door. The next morning, just before the Ukrainian carpenter was to cement the formica, he tried to send Jacob to the coffee shop.

"I'm sorry," Jake said, "I can't go now. I've got terrible problems in my stomach. I'll go to the coffee shop later."

He went to the bathroom, stood on the seat, and with the eraser side of a pencil pulled both calendars away from the hole. He watched and in ten minutes he learned the secret. Soon Mr. Goldstein gave him a raise because Jake was such a good worker. The Ukrainian wasn't the only one who could install Formica.

Jake took other formica jobs after hours. He would call to say he wouldn't be home for dinner for an hour or two. I never complained: why should I? He was working for David and me. So I told him, "Fine," and if I was grilling a steak, I made it into pot roast.

We get new quarters

For eight months we had to share our little apartment with Barbara and Herman. We each had a baby and they were growing bigger. We needed more space, but apartments were still very scarce. The landlord told me about another apartment that was going to become vacant, but we would have to pay him $500 under the table. We paid it and moved in. Our new apartment had three small rooms which were dark because the windows looked out onto a courtyard, but at least we had the place to ourselves.

Then came the cockroaches. We didn't know how to get rid of them. A little while later, while Jake was installing some cabinets in a restaurant, he saw some exterminators working. He told them about our cockroaches, and they gave him a can of the fluid they used.

"Put a capful in a bucket of water," they told him. Jake took the whole can and poured it all over the apartment. We had to leave the apartment for a whole day, but we never had any more cockroaches. They left our apartment and moved into all the others. The neighbors complained that they had never seen so many cockroaches.

"Where are they coming from?" they asked. There were 48 other tenants in the building. We knew, but we didn't say anything.

Our apartment was the cleanest in the building. Whenever the landlord wanted to show an apartment to possible tenants, he used ours.

Spring Valley, 1947

We rented a bungalow during the summer, because New York City was too hot and dusty. Jake would come on the weekend.

Jake gets a raise

My Uncle Sam asked Jake how much Goldstein paid him.

"Goldstein is cheating you," Sam said. "You're worth much more — you're not an apprentice — you're a skilled carpenter. Now I'll tell you what: I'll buy you wood and you build me a wardrobe."

So Jacob built a beautiful piece of furniture, with a place for suits, and shelves for shirts, underwear, and socks. Sam was delighted.

"You know what? Now I'll call Goldstein."

Immediately, he telephoned.

"Goldstein," he said, "how come you pay my nephew Jacob so little? Do you know he's not only a skilled carpenter but also an artist? I could find him a job right now at three times the money."

Goldstein tripled Jacob's weekly pay.

In 1949, Jake's brother Joseph, his wife Sally, and their son Irving joined us. Jake asked Mr. Goldstein to give him a job. "I will," he said, "but I can't pay him what you're getting."

In addition to working for Goldstein, Jake used to do some work on the side. Once he brought home some very thin plywood to make into a curved shelf for a jewelry display. It was very tricky to work with that plywood all by himself. But I was sick with a high temperature, and he didn't want to disturb me. After a while I sensed that he needed my help. I got out of bed to help him. I held the plywood while he nailed it. I saw tears in his eyes; he was so grateful for my love.

Jake and Joe go into business for themselves

Two weeks before Christmas, Goldstein fired Max, a devoted carpenter who had worked with Goldstein for over twenty years. Business was slow and Goldstein wanted to get rid of him. Right away, Jake gave Goldstein two-week's notice.

"If he can let a man go after twenty years to avoid paying him a bonus," Jake said, "how can I trust him?"

Joe Suss also gave Goldstein notice.

"Look for a place," Jake told me. "Joe and I will go into business for ourselves."

"But you don't speak good enough English, either of you," I said. "How are you going to work with customers?"

"Not a problem," Jacob said. And it wasn't. When someone called with an inquiry, Jacob would ask over the phone, "Do you speak Yiddish, German, Polish, Russian, or Ukrainian?" If the answer was no, Jacob would say, "Sorry, we can't do business together."

Sure enough, while Joe's wife Sally and I were walking David, we found a big basement to rent just a block away. Within a month, Joseph and Jacob had their own workshop, Suss Brothers. That was in January 1951.

We decide to have another child

The business was doing very well and we were very comfortable in our New York apartment. David was growing up nicely. Although we were very happy with our son, we did not want to have any more children. After all that we had suffered, especially seeing what Hitler had done to Jewish babies, we didn't want to bring any more children into the world.

One day while we were eating dinner David, who by this time was five years old, said, "Mommy, Daddy, I have been thinking. When I grow older I will be all alone in the world. I have no grandmas, no grandpas, no sisters or brothers. Why don't you go to the hospital and buy me a brother or sister?"

Jake and I looked at one another and said. "The kid is right."

Nine months a later, on April 25, 1953, we had a second son, Teddy, named after Jake's mother Tobi. I bless David every single day since then for opening our eyes.

David goes to kindergarten

The following September David entered kindergarten. He was so excited to go to school that first day, but when I came to pick him up, he was in tears.

"David, why you crying?" I asked.

"How come everyone has grandmas and grandpas?" he said. "Where are mine?"

We never discussed the war in front of him, so he had no idea. I was thinking what kind of answer to give him.

I didn't lie, but I didn't tell him the truth either. Why tell him that the Germans killed them? How would he react? Why should he be taught to hate?

They are in heaven," I answered. "When you grow older, you will find out." He seemed satisfied with that answer.

We move to Rochester, New York

My sister Barbara and her husband Herman moved to Rochester to work in a bakery that Jake's cousins had bought. My sister called and asked to visit me. She told me how much she missed me.

Now Jake and his brother had a very good Formica business in Manhattan, but that didn't matter.

"After all that you and Barbara have gone through together," he said, "you two sisters shouldn't be separated in a free country." So Jake sold his share of the business to Joe, and we moved to Rochester.

At first Jake found a few jobs working for other people in Rochester, but it wasn't long before he opened his own business, Jacob Suss, Incorporated, first on Clinton Avenue and then on 342 Norton Street. We found an apartment on Catherine Street, which I loved. It had big windows and was so bright after our New York apartment. But the neighbors were a problem. Every night they fought, using horrible language. It sounded as if they were going to kill each other. Immediately, we looked for something else.

I telephoned a woman who was advertising a three-bedroom apartment. She wanted to know if we had any children. I told her, "Yes, we have a boy of seven and another, a baby, twelve months old."

"I'm sorry," she said. "We don't want to rent to people with children."

I was shocked. I'd never heard such a thing before. Here in the United States, in a free country, they don't want to have people with children. I cried my eyes out.

"All right," Jacob said when I told him. "We'll buy our own house."

That was the start. We bought a two-family house on Van Stallen Street. The rent paid most of our mortgage. We had to pay only $10 more a month.

The business did well. David and Teddy were happy in school. We saw a lot of Barbara and Herman, their daughters and son. We had a lot of friends in the community. Jake became president of our temple, B'nai Israel.

June 1956

Jake, David, Teddy and me, in front of our two-family house on Van Stallen Street, Rochester. I'm wearing a tomato colored skirt and shawl, and a white blouse with matching embroidery. Of course, I made the whole outfit myself.

Our family celebrates another milestone.

Ted's Bar Mitzvah was held on May 7, 1966.
Like David's Bar Mitzvah before him we had 300 people attend.
At midnight Ted played My Yiddishe Momma *on the accordion*
because it was Mother's Day. He had been practicing for three
months. We all cried. Teddy too.

Nightmares

In Rochester we were flourishing, but there was one problem. I still had terrible nightmares. Every night I would be afraid to go to sleep. I would always dream that I was hiding in an attic, holding my baby. The Germans were chasing me and wanted to take my baby away. I would start to scream.

Night after night, Jake would wake me up and try to comfort me. "It's over now," he said. "You're in America now and safe. Our children are safe. Go back to sleep."

But the nightmares wouldn't go away. One night I dreamt about Motus. He was talking to me.

"I'm alone. I'm sick. I can't live without you."

"Tell me where you are," I said, "and I'll come to you."

His voice faded.

"Where are you?" I called out to him. I saw his lips moving, but I couldn't make out his words. Again Jake woke me up, but the dream was always in the back of my mind. It comes back to me now as I tell the story. There's no closure to this grief. This sense of loss — for Motus, for my father, for my mother — will be with me as long as I live.

In February 1969, we went to Tucson, Arizona, to visit cousins. We had booked a hotel, but Jake's cousin met us at the airport.

"I've cancelled your booking," he said. "You're not staying at any hotel. We've lots of room; you'll stay with us."

We had a wonderful month in the sun.

Back in Rochester at the beginning of March, we went for our yearly physicals. At that time the doctor would take chest x-rays. It was the day before Purim and there was going to be a party at our temple. Jake meant to call the doctor's office to find out the results, but we were very busy planning the Purim party, and he forgot. On Monday he asked me to call.

"Jake's x-rays didn't come out so well," the doctor told me. "I want him to come back for another x-ray." The doctor knew that something was wrong, but he didn't want to scare us on the phone.

Jake had another set of x-rays taken. This time they found a spot on his lung. How could this be? After Arizona he had looked fine. There were no outward signs. He didn't have any pain.

He went into St. Mary's Hospital for an exploratory operation. They found cancer— it had spread all over his body. He had only a short time to live. He knew it and I knew it. We told David. Only Ted didn't know.

Passover

Jake was still in St. Mary's Hospital recovering from the operation when Passover arrived. I asked the head nurse if it would be all right if I made a Seder in his room. She asked the doctor who said, "Sure, why not?" So I prepared a Seder. I went home and cooked the entire meal. David, Ted and I came to the hospital and sat around the square bridge table that I had brought. We read from our Passover *Haggadah*. Jacob started to make the blessing over the wine, but after one sentence, he turned to David to go on. He hadn't the strength to continue.

It was Jacob's last Seder; he knew it, I knew it, David knew it. Only Ted didn't know. He had exams coming up and I didn't want him to be upset.

I have a photograph of that Seder. There is Jake, with a big smile on his face as usual. I'm smiling, too, but it was just a lie. We both knew he wouldn't last long.

The doctors, not able to do anything more for Jake, sent him home. He went back and forth to the hospital. But by the middle of June, the pain was too much for him, so he went back into St. Mary's Hospital. After I helped him get settled into his room, I started packing up his clothes to take with me.

"How come you're not leaving Daddy's clothes for him to come home in?" Ted asked.

Then I told him. "Daddy won't be coming home, Ted. He has cancer and they can't do anything to save him."

Ted just sat there without moving. "Why didn't you tell me?" he asked.

"I didn't want you to be distracted from your exams," I said.

On June 27, 1969, Jake died. We had been married 23 years, three months, and three days. He was 57 years old, a young man. At the age of 46, I was left a widow, with two sons.

This was a terrible blow, the most terrible of my life. For months I was numb. I looked after the boys, I kept house, but on the inside I was dead. Finally, to keep myself busy I began to work at Malek's Bakery. I had to get up at 4 o'clock every morning, but it helped stop me from thinking.

After all I had gone through, the murder of my mother at Chelmno, the murder of my father and Motus at Auschwitz, this was the hardest. And you know what? It still is.

Last seder at the hospital

My nightmares stop

Right after Jake passed away, my nightmares stopped. I asked Henry, a friend of ours, "How come when Jake was alive, he had to wake me almost every night because I had nightmares. Now that he has passed away, the nightmares have stopped."

"Jake loved you very much," he replied. "He wanted you to lead a normal life so when he died he took all your nightmares with him." And from that time I never had another nightmare.

Angel

Night after night, her husband, also a survivor,
woke to her terrors — children brained against walls,
her parents murdered, barracks squeezing her
into unconsciousness—but since the day he died,
she has never dreamed another nightmare,
he took them all with him, so brave his soul,
so much did he love her, so much does he love her still.

William Heyen

Epilogue

Two years ago, I visited the United States Memorial Holocaust Museum in Washington with a group of teachers. I found out that on the fifth floor they have a room with records, which lists all the people from Lodz who were murdered. I knew I could find out what happened to my mother, to my father and Motus. They have a book with all the names in it. All I had to do was open it.

I couldn't. I froze. I couldn't bring myself to go to that room.

The next year, I went to the Museum again with another group of teachers. Again I found my way to the room with the Lodz records. "This time," I thought, "I'll open it and find out."

Again, I froze. I couldn't bring myself to do it. I still can't.

When I came to Nazareth College to speak to Dr. Susan Nowak's Auschwitz and After class, one of the students I met was Kelly Ceckowski. Her great, great grandfather had come to the United States from Poland in the 1920's. Kelly was tall and thin with light brown hair and fair skin. She looks Polish. I was introduced to Kelly's family and we became special friends.

Kelly came with me when I accompanied a group of Brockport College students to the United States Holocaust Memorial Museum. We went through the permanent exhibit together and then we sat in the Hall of Remembrance. I thought about all the members of my family who had been murdered: my father, mother, brother, aunts, uncles and cousins. I wept and Kelly wept with me. I lit a candle for them.

For her final project at Nazareth, Kelly, an art education major, designed a beautiful children's book about my life. She illustrated it with photographs of my family, my grandparents and parents, my brother Motus, and Bronya and me before the Holocaust. She bound it by hand, having it open from left to right as if it were a Hebrew book. She called it *Angie's Story*. The book is a work of art, which I shall always treasure. I'll leave it in my will to my grandchildren.

In May 2001 Kelly was one of fourteen Nazareth College students chosen from students all over the United States to go to Poland on the

March of Remembrance and Hope. They visited places where Jews once lived and died. She toured some concentration camps.

When she visited Auschwitz, she lit a remembrance candle, which she had prepared. She had engraved our family name, *Szpilman* on it. She took a photograph of that burning candle and brought it back to me. She knew I would never return to Auschwitz, or Poland, for that matter. So she made this pilgrimage for me. Kelly was trying to heal the wound in my heart.

She brought me another gift, a little wooden box, hand-engraved in Poland. In it were two pebbles from the mass grave where she lit the candle, the two matches she used to light the candle, and a slip of paper that read, Remembrance and Hope.

This young Polish-American girl showed me that we are all God's children. Kelly believes this deeply, and so do I. If you hold something like that in your heart, you have hope, and you give hope.

Afterword by Dr. Martin Rumscheidt

Dr. Martin Rumscheidt, Professor of Theology at Charles University, was a child of the Nazi regime. He has spent a lifetime exploring questions of guilt and repentance, mourning and reconciliation. Dr. Rumscheidt came to Rochester in April 2002 to speak at Nazareth College's Holocaust Remembrance Day ceremony. Prior to that he had attended both the community commemoration of Yom Hashoah and an interschool commemoration where he heard Angie address hundreds of school-aged children. Angie's words moved him deeply. Here are his reflections.

It was a Tuesday morning in Rochester. The previous evening, many people had gathered in the large auditorium of the Jewish Community Center to remember the millions —children, women and men, the old, those in their prime and those with their future still before them, whom the Nazis and their collaborators had murdered in what is now known as the Shoah. This auditorium was now filled with schoolchildren and their teachers who gathered to hear the testimony of a woman who survived those atrocities, first in the ghetto, then in Auschwitz and, finally, in a slave labor camp. The room was still laden with the prayers, sighs and songs of the night before, with bitter memories but also the joy of an ongoing and flourishing Jewish life in various parts of the world. It was for me as if I could still hear the *shofar's* sounds, imploring God for the peace of Jerusalem, of Israel.

I was introduced to Anna Suss Paull, Angie, or Andzia, as her name is rendered in affectionate Polish terms. She is a "petite" woman, as Canadians would put it, with a gentle and warm expression in her face. When she began to speak, I became—literally—all ears and could not take my eyes off her, to mix my metaphor. She spoke with ease while the substance she reported was brimming over with the cruelty, mendacity, disdain and rage of the Germans who, with their "helpers," were carrying out the process of eradicating Jews from Europe. I wondered whether any of my relatives and friends' parents had been among the murderers. Yet, I was touched at a deeper, directly personal level by Andzia's words. It was not what she said but how she expressed her burden of horror which made something happen in me.

That afternoon I made a presentation for a Yom Hashoah commemoration at Nazareth College and was able to find words to tell what had happened to me.

"I fell in love this morning," I said, " with a woman who is now in this room. Andzia, I hope that you will allow me to put it this way. As you spoke to those school children, you also spoke directly to me and frequently looked me in the eyes. It was then I realized that the meticulous and incessant teaching I had received in my school, church and, more indirectly perhaps, in my home between 1939 and 1945 had not utterly melted away but had gone 'underground' or 'into hiding' somewhere within me. I had believed I had overcome the teaching that Jews where 'subhuman,' that Slavs were just somewhat less 'subhuman' than Jews, and that someone Jewish and Polish was radically 'subhuman.' At the level of intellect or rationality, I had indeed dealt with this ideological perversity, rejecting and condemning it altogether. But you, Andzia, did not speak to my brain but to my whole being and its deepest recesses. And there your words found the hidden serpent. There your gentle and strong humanity, free of hate and vengeance, called me to become free from an old, long-borne burden that I had thought I had thrown off. You lifted it from me with your words, your story, your humanity. And so, Andzia, you redeemed me from something that, in its quiet unconscious manner, had clung to me, waiting perhaps, to find occasion to poison me anew. I thank you from my heart, in ways that I cannot express, for the liberation you brought this day into my life."

When Angie embraced me a few moments later, it felt as if the little boy Martin was facing the just a bit older and wiser Andzia Szpilman of Lodz. She wanted him to go forward into life without hate. Free of the lies his family, nation and church were about to teach him.

"You, Andzia, are and will be a beloved companion to me whose hands I gratefully hold and won't let go as long as I have breath."

Artist's Statement

Deborah A. DiFilippo lives with her husband in Rochester, NY, where she directs faith formation at an urban Catholic parish. She has a bachelor's degree in Religious Studies from Nazareth College where she first met Angie Suss Paull.

I had always shied away from stories about the Holocaust, feeling it is all too horrendous to think about. I dismissed it with such thoughts as: "I don't need to hear about all that. I know it was bad. It's all too disturbing. Besides, I would never persecute a whole culture, so why should I have to know about it and get upset over it?"

And then I met Angie Suss Paull and heard her tell her story.

I realized then that we cannot turn a blind eye to the evil and injustice in this world just because it's too disturbing to think about. We *must* learn and not allow history to repeat itself.

Angie came to America, and despite well-intentioned advice from caring people to "forget it all now – it's past," she refuses to forget the horror, lest she also forget her family and those who did not survive. Nothing can be gained by the silence of the survivors of the Shoah – a great deal can be lost by their silence. We must know their stories, especially the ones that show courageous examples of retaining one's sense of humanness in situations that try to destroy it. Their stories also teach us to be constantly vigilant, not to get caught up in the business of hatred, prejudice, scapegoating, and persecution.

Angie has been successful in her resolution not to raise her two sons to continue the hatred and "become barbarians" like those who tried to destroy her and the spirituality that has sustained her throughout our life. A light shines through Angie that expresses humanity at its best. This she has passed down to a new generation.

My collage, while portraying the devastating loss of life, will call to mind that against great odds, people like Angie somehow held onto their sense of humanity, their belief in God, and managed to act compassionately whenever it was possible.

Some symbolism in the collage:

- The distorted Star of David represents the distortion of Judaism by the Nazis and antisemitism throughout history
- The white cloth represents one of Angie's miracles. Her sister was saved from a selection when a small piece of white cloth fell from the sky. Angie used the cloth to wipe away evidence of a blemish on her sister's face.
- The photo of Angie's brother commemorating his Bar Mitzvah was the one photo that touched me the deepest and prompted me to learn more about the Shoah. The hope and promise of this young man, like so many others, was snuffed out by hatred.
- I considered tearing the photo of Angie and her sister (who also survived) and her mother and brother (who did not) in half, dividing the survivors from those who didn't as a symbol of how the Nazis tore families apart. I decided against it. Psychologically I couldn't bring myself to tear the photo. Besides, Angie's story keeps the memory of her family intact; it should stay whole.
- The hands in the center can be seen as grabbing or as sharing. My understanding of Jewish resistance during the Shoah is in their retaining a sense of humanity even against great odds. The space in the hands is ambiguously blank, open to the interpretation of the viewer.
- The bridge was painted from a photo of one in the Lodz ghetto. Bridges usually symbolize connections; this one was built by the Nazis to separate the Jews from the rest of society. The placement of the bridge in this composition moves Angie from one part of her life to another.
- The destroyed synagogue is not the Lodz synagogue pictured burning in the book, but is the Fasanenstrasse Synagogue in Berlin, torn apart by antisemitic mobs during Kristallnacht. I used this synagogue to demonstrate the magnitude of the destruction and the frightening violence incited by the government and perpetrated against Jews by mobs of their fellow citizens.
- Angie and her son are depicted leaving Europe for American and symbolize a renewed hope for the future.
- The necklace Angie always wears is one of her few remaining physical links to her parents and their love; it is also a link to her ancestry.

Testimonies and Letters from Family Members

David Suss, Angie's son

I often speak about my parents and what I know of their life experiences, including the unthinkable tragedies they endured and the challenges they faced before, during and after the Holocaust. Most of these discussions have taken place with family and friends in social or holiday settings, and there was always a level of disbelief whenever I attempted to describe some of the vivid details of their lives.

This is my first attempt at sharing, in writing, my own perceptions and recollections of what it meant to be the child of Holocaust survivors. Many others, far more eloquent and insightful than I, have penned wonderfully descriptive and informative recollections of their adolescent years. They have successfully portrayed the way their families overcame the hurt, obstacles and culture shock associated with the premature death of loved ones and the anguish of losing all of their possessions coupled with the need to relocate to new and unfamiliar parts of the world.

For me, life as a young child was really very simple. I did not know that my parents were learning to speak a new language nor did I have any awareness that we were immigrants in New York City. Because it was such a melting pot of diverse cultures, everyone was different in their own way but everyone was very cognizant of and devoted to their individual roots. My own personal English speaking skills didn't really fully develop until kindergarten when other students chuckled and told me that I "talked funny." Since learning was to be my primary focus as a youth, this problem was quickly overcome.

As I reached my adolescent years, I knew that my knowledge of the language was greater than that of my parents. In a sense, I became their mentor by often helping my father with business correspondence and helping my mother with sentence structure. The realization that I was helping them with their homework gave me great personal satisfaction as I began to understand why they were unable to complete their formal education. It would have been nice for me to be able to rely on my parents to assist me with math, science or social studies but that was not to be. On occasion, the burden of being the educational household resource would frustrate me, but my parents made up for that in many ways. The education they each gave me when it came to values, common sense and decency was immeasurable and I doubt that any of my peers came close to the lessons I was able to learn from them.

I have been blessed with the privilege of having two marvelous parents. My father, who died in 1969, left me with a legacy of a strong work ethic, importance of family, the need to give back the community and, my personal favorite, a keen sense of humor. To this day, I continually use many of his European expressions and anecdotes to both amuse and provide lessons to those I know. He was particularly proud of my Bar Mitzvah and my high school and college graduations. Having been denied education past the third grade, his pride was evident watching his son complete his studies and receive his diploma. This is why he came to American and why he cherished his freedom here. The Bar Mitzvah joy was focused on the fact that he survived Nazi persecution and was able to see his first-born reach a Jewish milestone that so many others were denied during the Holocaust. He often remarked that he would never knowingly miss attending a joyous occasion. He reasoned that people always seemed to make time to attend funerals so why shouldn't the same effort be made for a happy event.

My mother, who has been amazingly supportive throughout my life, is truly a profile in courage. Having persevered and miraculously surviving the atrocities inflicted on her and her family, she was the consummate mother. Her focus has always been her family and tending to their needs. Beyond the traditional chores of cooking, cleaning, sewing and running a household, she was supportive of my father's efforts when it came to providing for the family. She never complained about the long hours he had to work and accepted his time away from home as a necessity for our survival. After he started his own business, my mother assisted him with secretarial work, bill paying, running errands and, to my own personal amazement, painting and varnishing much of the cabinetry my father built. They made an inseparable team and could anticipate the other's move merely by glancing at one another.

For almost 16 years, she has channeled her energy into teaching others about the human side of the Holocaust. By visiting schools and lecturing to various civic, educational and social groups, she has provided her personal knowledge of what it was like to encounter the wrath of hate and the behavior of demons. While her story details much of her existence throughout the war, it does not begin to tell the bravery and courage that she exhibited for six very long years. To say I am proud would be an understatement, but I cannot think of a better word to describe her tenacity and her conviction in attempting to reach as many people as she can through her frequent appearances as a speaker.

It is with great honor and great humility that I dedicate these few words to her and, on behalf of all the members of my family, thank her for all she has done. May God bless her and may she always know that I love her very much.

Appendix B

Ted Suss, Angie's son

Being the son of two Holocaust survivors, my childhood was very different from that of most Americans. I never knew my grandparents or many of my aunts and uncles. My parents had an entirely differently life-style and outlook. They led a very simple life where family and friends were always their priority. Living to see both sons celebrate their Bar Mitzvahs was the ultimate highlight.

My mother, Angie, survived the war and has outlived two husbands. Her children and grandchildren (whom my father didn't live to see) are the most important people in her life.

Unlike many Holocaust survivors who kept their experiences and feelings to themselves, my Mom shared some of her stories with my brother David and me, from a very young age. Later in my life, I realized the Holocaust had taken place only 15 years earlier. We were always aware of that time in her life, but not until I was older and more mature, did I fully realize the impact it had on her. Being a young child, it all seemed like something in history, not something that was real.

My mom has been speaking to students about her experiences during the Holocaust for many years. She feels that one reason her life was spared is to share her story so others will know that it was real, and to make sure no one ever forgets. I am so proud to be Angie's son.

Appendix C

My Hero: Angie Suss Paull
By Jake Suss, sixth grade

My grandmother, Angie Suss Paull (Andzia Szpilman) was born in 1922 in Lodz, Poland and now lives in Rochester, New York. She travels back and forth from Rochester to Palm Springs, California, where one of her two sons, David Suss, lives. Her other son, Ted Suss, my dad, lives here in Northbrook, Illinois. My grandmother, along with her family, experienced the horrors of the Holocaust. She saved her sister's life twice during this horrendous war.

Angie's family was not so big. She had a father, a mother, a sister and a brother. Her mother Lea was taken away from the family in the ghetto in 1942. Her father David and her brother Motus were killed two days after their arrival in Auschwitz. Her sister Barbara survived the war and lives in Rochester today.

Angie's husband, my grandfather Jacob Suss, was also a survivor of the Holocaust. At the end of the war when the Germans were shooting all the prisoners on a death march, my grandfather was lucky and got shot through the nose instead. He played dead and was freed. Jacob and Andzia met in Germany in a displaced persons camp where he asked her to marry him six days later. They got married on March 24, 1945. Their son, David Suss, was born on June 2, 1947, and they came to America in December of 1947. Their son Ted Suss was born in New York on April 25, 1953.

During the war, Angie saved her sister Barbara's life twice. One time they were on a train jam packed with girls going to a camp. The train stopped very hard, throwing all of them on the floor, injuring some of them. Barbara was one of the injured. The Nazis took the few injured into care. Angie saw them put the medicine on her injured ankle, but she noticed they did not clean it first. So obviously they did not care. Angie overheard the Nazis talking. They were saying, "Why do we have to take care of them anyways, they will be gone by the morning?" Angie waited for the Nazis to leave, and then went up to Barbara and said,

"We have to go!" She said, "No, no I have this comfortable bed and I don't want to leave." Angie made her leave anyways. Both of them went to check on who was there the next day, but everyone was gone. Angie was right.

The second time she saved Barbara was when they were standing in line to be checked. If anything was wrong, you would be killed. Nothing was wrong with Angie, but Barbara had a pimple on her face. Sadly that was enough to get her killed. As Angie tells it, "a cloth fell from the sky into my hands." She had a plan. When they got up to be checked, she pushed and swiped across the pimple as hard as she could. The pimple turned white as her skin, and the Nazis luckily did not notice. That is how she saved her life, twice.

Angie is writing a book that is going to come out in the fall. Her book is going to be called *Angie's Story*. It is about her life before, during, and after the war. She told her story to Barbara Appelbaum and a college professor named Peter Marchant. They wrote the book with her.

I chose my grandmother to be my hero because she has gone through the war and acts like an everyday person. She volunteers to speak at schools instead of hiding it in herself because she believes that she should share with kids, from junior to senior high school, so they know how it happened and that it doesn't happen again.

This is why she is my hero.

Reply to Jake: Peter Marchant

Dear Jake:

Your grandmother showed me your essay on "My Hero." It moved her to tears, tears of joy and pride. With good reason: your essay is excellent, both in content and form. The writing is really good, and the material comes from your heart.

You know that Barbara Appelbaum, the director of the Center for Holocaust Awareness and Information of the Jewish Federation of Greater Rochester, and I have been working on *Angie's Story* for seven years, trying to capture something of your grandmother's and grandfather's story. It has not been easy. And now you have managed to put on paper the essence of Angie, and of your grandfather and namesake, Jacob Suss.

I never met your grandfather, but through your grandmother it is as if I knew him myself. He was an extraordinary man, clever, brave, tough, sensitive, and generous of spirit. Yes, indeed, a hero.

Your grandmother, Angie, has told me stories that I hope never to forget of how the Szpilman family survived in the terrible conditions of the Litzmannstadt Ghetto, and managed to remain loving and essentially civilized when many others, understandably, had reverted to animal selfishness.

Your grandmother has come to talk to every class I've had on the Literature of the Holocaust since 1993, that is two or even three classes a year, about 750 students in all. This is just one college course. She goes to middle schools and high schools all through the area, and in Palm Springs, California, too. She is always a favorite. She makes her audiences feel a part of what she went through. Sometimes they cry, sometimes, because she makes them, they laugh, and often they remember. She brings the appalling and unimaginable statistics of the Holocaust to life, and those who hear her are touched to the heart.

Why does she do all this work? Why does she put herself through these most painful experiences over and over again? So that those who never experienced the horrors of the Shoah will understand something of it, and feel it as living history from which they can learn.

What she has to teach is important: don't complain and feel sorry for yourself. Accept what has to be accepted, hunger, cold and danger. Don't dwell on the happiness you have lost. Don't allow anger and the desire for revenge to destroy you. Don't stand by and watch people in pain and trouble and do nothing: do what you can to help. Never allow yourself to lose hope.

Part of the joy your grandmother gets from your essay is to know that her story, and your grandfather Jacob's story, are alive to you: she sees that you will learn the sort of people they come from, and be proud. That's the reason for *Angie's Story*, the book we've been laboring over for all these years. Your essay gives us a sense of hope that their story will not be forgotten.

You did a great job.

Sincerely,
Peter Marchant
Professor Emeritus of English
SUNY Brockport

NOTES

1. Warsaw had the largest Jewish population in Europe; Lodz had the second largest. *Concise Statistical Year-Book of Poland*: Sept. 1939-June 1941 as quoted in Lucjan Dobroszycki, ed., *The Chronicle of the Lodz Ghetto 1941-1944*, trans. Richard Lourie and Joachim Neugroschel (Binghamton: Vail-Ballou, 1984), xxx.

2. The Germans occupied Lodz on September 8, 1939. "Lodz." *Encyclopaedia Judaica.* 1972 or 1978, 432.

3. After the Nazis had overrun Poland, some areas were annexed into the Third Reich and became completely under German control. Lodz was incorporated into the Third Reich and was forced to lose its Polish and Jewish identities and became Germanized. German became the official language and even the city's name was changed to Litzmannstadt. Lucjan Dobroszycki, ed., *The Chronicle of the Lodz Ghetto* 1941-1944, trans. Richard Lourie and Joachim Neugroschel (Binghamton: Vail-Ballou, 1984), xxiii.

4. The Nazis continued to cause terror by destroying the major synagogues of Lodz one year after the violence of Kristallnacht, the night of broken glass, in November 1938. Lucjan Dobroszycki, ed., *The Chronicle of the Lodz Ghetto*, xxxiv.

5. Jews early on were forced to wear armbands with the star of David. Later patches were worn. *Deutsche Lodzer Zeitung*, a German newspaper that published decrees, as quoted in *The Chronicle of the Lodz Ghetto*, xxxiii.

6. Jews had to be off the street by 7 pm until 8 am. *Deutsche Lodzer Zeitung*, a German newspaper that published decrees, as quoted in *The Chronicle of the Lodz Ghetto*, xxxiii.

7. Wireless radios had to be turned over to authorities, thus it was difficult to find out information about the war. *Deutsche Lodzer Zeitung*, a German newspaper that published decrees, as quoted in *The Chronicle of the Lodz Ghetto,* xxxiii.

8. The Kripo, or criminal police, was located within the Lodz Ghetto. They had taken over a Christian church and converted it into their headquarters with the prison in the cellars. *The Chronicle of the Lodz Ghetto*, xxxix.

9. About 164,000 Jews were sealed in the ghetto. Over 70,000 had left or fled in hopes of escape prior to its closing. "Lodz." *Encyclopaedia Judaica.* 1972 or 1978, 433.

10. Unlike the Warsaw Ghetto the Lodz Ghetto was completely cut off from the rest of the Germanized city and the rest of Europe, The Jews of Lodz could not trade or exchange contact with anyone on the "Aryan" side. Jews were not able to leave or escape through the barbed wire fences or gates. The inhabitants were totally secluded and imprisoned.

11. The Nazis set the provisioning level for the ghetto population at one half the per-capita norm for inmates of German prisons. Hans Biebow, the German overseer, rightly assumed that the Jews would part with all their valuable possessions to stave off hunger, and thereafter they would have to earn their meager keep through slave labor in one of the ghetto industries – or perish. Alan Adelson and Robert Lapides, ed. *The Lodz Ghetto* (New York: Penguin Group, 1989), xviii.

12. Rations included horsemeat sausage. Michal Unger, ed., *The Last Ghetto: Life in the Lodz Ghetto* 1940-1944 (Jerusalem: Ahva Coop. Printing Press, 1995), 97.

13. During the "Sperra" in September 1942, Germans searched the ghetto during this time period for the ill, elderly and children who were to be deported. Michal Unger, ed., *The Last Ghetto: Life in the Lodz Ghetto* 1940-1944 (Jerusalem: Ahva Coop. Printing Press, 1995), 79.

14. Chelmno was intended to be the extermination camp for the Lodz Ghetto. It was also the first camp in which poisonous gas was used for killing, 80-82. From March 1943 until June 1944, transports to Chelmno stopped. However, in June 1944, the Germans decided that the Lodz Ghetto must be liquidated and gassings continued at Chelmno.

15. Due to the threat of the advancing Soviet Army, extermination ceased in mid-July 1944 at Chelmno. Yet, liquidation continued and Jews were sent to Auschwitz. *The Chronicle of the Lodz Ghetto*, lxiii-lxv.

16. 877 people survived who had stayed behind to help with cleanup or went into hiding and escaped later deportations. The Russians liberated the Lodz Ghetto in January 1945. Bendet Hershkovitch as quoted in, *The Chronicle of the Lodz Ghetto*, lxvi.

17. Bergen-Belsen had been divided into eight different prisoner camp sections, *Historical Atlas on the Holocaust*, 165.

18. Salzwedel was located about 50 miles east from Bergen-Belsen concentration camp. *Historical Atlas on the Holocaust*, 209.

19. Landsberg-am-Lach was a Dachau subcamp and it was liberated in April 1945. It later became a displaced persons camp under United States occupation in southern Germany. By the end of 1946 there were approximately 250,000 Jewish displaced persons in Europe. *Historical Atlas on the Holocaust*, 146, 209, 217.

Photographic Credits:

- Page 12: "Temple Burning" The burning of the Reform Synagogue on Kosciuszko Square in Lodz. The Halianate Synagogue was built in 1888. Beit Lohamei Haghettaot, courtesy of USHMM Photo Archives.
- Page 14: Family photograph of klezmer musicians courtesy of Angie Suss Paull.
- Page 16: Family photograph of family army band courtesy of Angie Suss Paull.
- Page 30: "Hanged Man" *Lodz Ghetto: Inside a Community Under Siege*; Alan Adelson, editor, courtesy of Jewish Heritage Project.
- Page 35: "Street Map of the Lodz Ghetto" *Lodz Ghetto: Inside a Community Under Siege*; Alan Adelson, editor, courtesy of Jewish Heritage Project.
- Page 36: "Starved Boy" A boy kneels in a doorway, his head resting on a soup pail. Written on the back in Yiddish, "He dreams about a soup." USHMM, courtesy of YIVO Institute.
- Page 39: "Straw Shoe Factory" *Lodz Ghetto: Inside a Community Under Siege*; Alan Adelson, editor, courtesy of Jewish Heritage Project.
- Page 45: "Bridge in Lodz Ghetto" View of the pedestriuan bridge over Zgierska Street At Koscielny Square in the Lodz ghetto. Below, a German photographer films the Jews crossing the bridge. Courtesy of Bundesarchiv.
- Page 45: "Boys Hauling Cart" Four children haul a heavily laden cart through the streets of the Lodz Ghetto. Beit Lohamei Haghettaot, courtesy of USHMM Photo Archives.
- Page 48: "Boy Saying Goodbye" A child who has been selected for deportation bids farewell to his family through the wire fence of the central prison, during the "Gehsperre" action in the Lodz ghetto. USHMM, courtesy of Beit Lohamei Haghettaot.
- Page 49: "Hospital Escape" Jewish police block the escape of the Jews from the hospital on Drewnowska Street, where they were being held temporarily until their deportation from the Lodz ghetto. USHMM, courtesy of YIVO Institute.
- Page 55: "Liquidation of the Ghetto" Jewish police escort a long column of Jews through Marysin towards the train station in Radogoszcz during a deportation action in the Lodz ghetto. Beit Lohamei Haghettaot, courtesy of USHMM Photo Archives.
- Page 58: "Deportation to Auschwitz, August 1944" *Lodz Ghetto: Inside a Community Under Siege*, courtesy of Jewish Heritage Project.

- Page 59: "Arbeit Macht Frei" View of the entrance to the main camp of Auschwitz (Auschwitz I). The gate bears the motto "Arbeit Macht Frei" (Work Makes One Free). USHMM, courtesy of Main Commission for the Prosecution of the Crimes against the Polish Nation.
- Page 63: "Interior of the Barracks at Birkenau" Courtesy of the Auschwitz State Museum.
- Page 64: "Latrines at Auschwitz" Courtesy of Panstwowe Muzeum Auschwitz-Birkenau w Oswiecimiu.
- Page 128: "Memorial Candle at Auschwitz," courtesy of Kelly Ceckowski.
- All family photographs courtesy of Angie Suss Paull.

Angie with her sister Barbara Mand

The Suss Family at the Bar Mitzvah of Erin and Corey Suss
April 4, 1998

Back row left to right: Jason, Jule, Erin, David, Nan and Ted
Front row left to right: Jake, Angie and Corey